P9-ELV-859

ORIGAMI

PAPERFOLDING FOR FUN

Eric Kenneway

OCTOPUS

CONTENTS

First published 1980 by Octopus Books Limited
59 Grosvenor Street, London W1

 ISBN 0 7064 1015 7

Produced by Mandarin Publishers Limited
22a Westlands Road, Quarry Bay, Hong Kong

Printed in Hong Kong

Photographs by Peter Rauter

INTRODUCTION

The ancient Chinese were the inventors of paper and discovered how to fold it; paperfolding with a purpose, however, originated in mediaeval Japan. It was a very formal kind of paperfolding with roots lying deep in folk religion and with a strictly ceremonial function; but out of this grew a kind of paperfolding more familiar to us – paperfolding as play. Ways of making birds, flowers and animals, simply by folding a sheet of paper, were passed down by Japanese mothers to their daughters for generations until modern times. The west had its traditional paper folds too, but, whereas in Japan paperfolding was for girls, in the west it was more often associated with boys; our well-known folds are things like boats, planes and soldiers' hats.

Nowadays paperfolding, dignified by its Japanese name *origami*, can be enjoyed by everybody. Paperfolding play has grown up. In recent decades an international origami movement has developed in which people of all ages and from very different backgrounds fold paper for pleasure. New and more complex ways of folding paper are being discovered; new subject matter is being attempted – but always the result is achieved simply by folding paper, without glueing, cutting, or stapling or using any other aid.

This book will introduce you to some of the recent exciting developments in origami and remind you of a few old favourites. Work through the projects in this book; then use the techniques you have learnt to discover the greater pleasure of creative origami.

For each of the projects in this book step-by-step instructions with diagrams are given. Each diagram shows the shape of the paper before the instruction is completed. When folding, look at the diagram, read the instruction, then look ahead to the next diagram to see what shape should result from that step's fold.

Try to fold neatly and accurately but do not be discouraged if your first attempts are not very successful. With more practice you will become familiar with the various ways in which paper behaves when it is folded and you will begin to see the limitless possibilities of this fascinating activity.

ADDRESSES

For further information about paper supplies, origami books, or news about origami activities in your area, contact one of the following:

British Origami Society
Mick Guy, Hon. Sec.
193 Abbey Road
Warley
Worcs.

Origami Center of America
Lillian Oppenheimer, Director
31 Union Square West
New York N.Y. 10003
U.S.A.

PAPER

You will find that most sorts of paper can be folded into origami models, but try several types and decide what suits you best. Packets of special origami paper, coloured on one side and white on the other, can now be obtained from many department stores, stationery shops, toy shops and oriental gift shops. Other suitable papers can be found in art and craft shops; and plain and fancy wrapping papers are widely available. If you want to get started and have no other material to hand, cut out a few pages from a colour magazine and try using these.

SYMBOLS

The following symbols are used throughout. Make sure that you understand them before reading further.

A) A line of dashes indicates a 'valley' fold – a concave crease. A solid arrow is generally used to indicate the direction of a fold.

B) A line of dots and dashes indicates a 'mountain' fold – a convex crease. A hollow-headed arrow is used when paper is folded to the rear of a model.

C) A looped arrow means 'Turn the paper over.'

D) An arrow headed at both ends means 'Fold, crease firmly and return the paper to its previous position.'

A faint line represents an existing crease line – one which is the result of a previous step.

A small circle means 'Hold the paper between finger and thumb.'

E) A solid arrow head means 'Press' or 'Push in'.

F) A hollow arrow means 'Pull out'.

G) A multi-curved arrow means 'Fold the paper over and over again.'

H) A swollen arrow indicates that the following diagram is drawn to a larger scale.

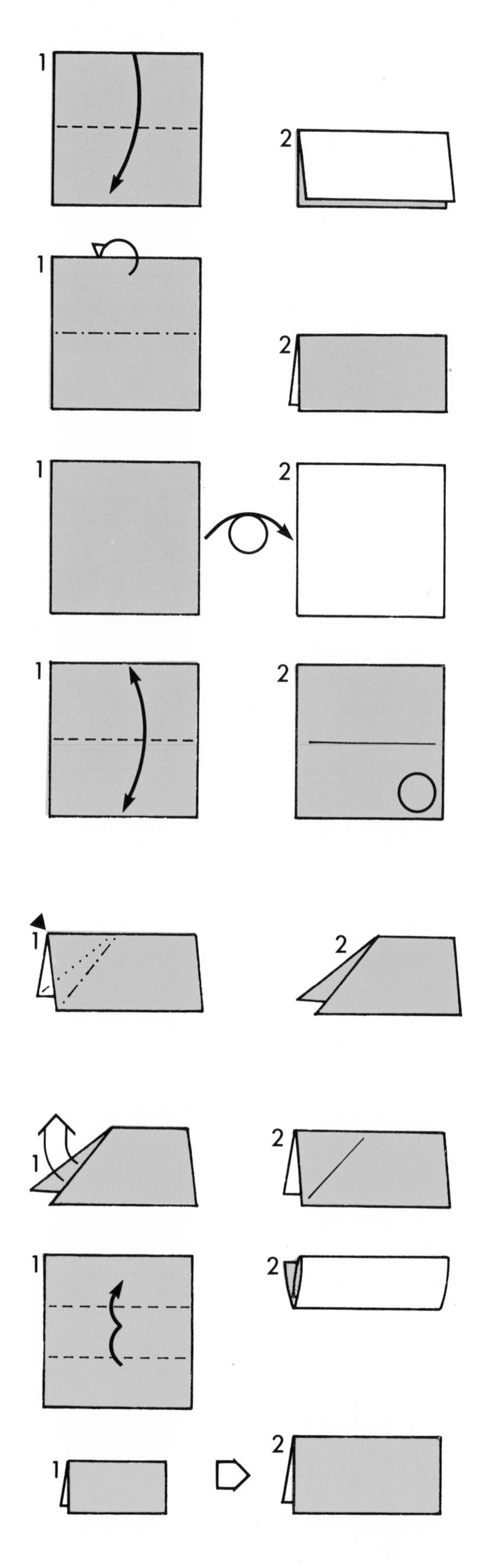

VOCABULARY AND PROCEDURES

You will find certain words and phrases recurring; these are the names of procedures – combinations of folds – which are frequently used in origami. It is by means of these procedures that we modify the shape of our paper, and create extra layers to be modified in turn, until the final shape is achieved.

Familiarity with origami procedures and an understanding of their effects is the key to successful creative folding.

Pleat Make parallel folds taking one section of paper behind, or in front of, another.

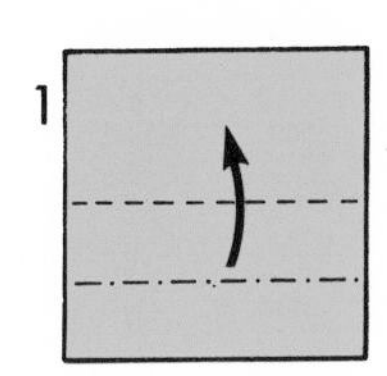

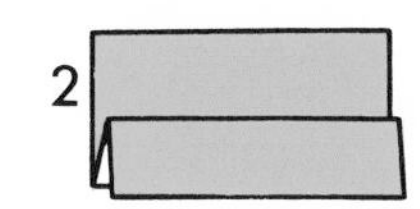

Swivel Make a pleat in which the folds meet at one edge.

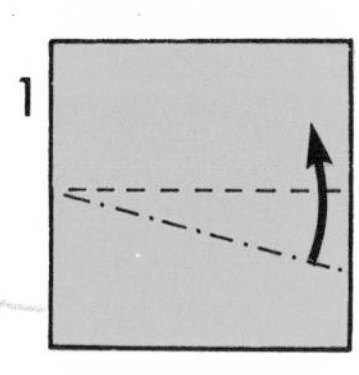

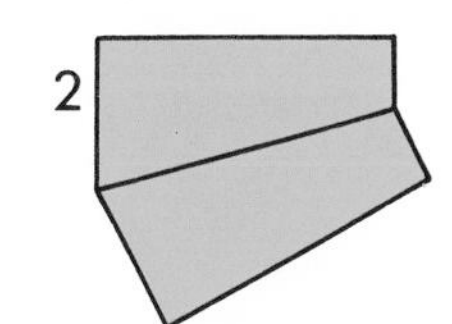

Inside reverse fold Reverse part of the folded edge – the spine – of a doubled sheet of paper between the two layers to form a trough.

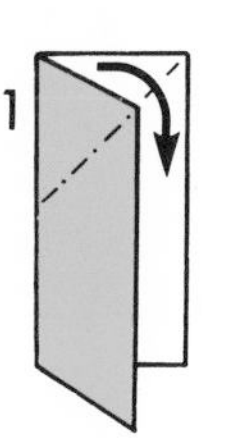

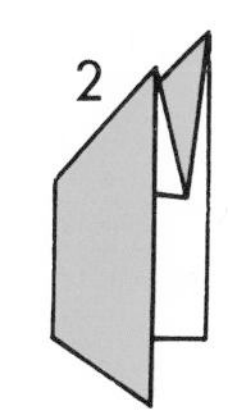

Outside reverse fold Reverse the folded edge of a doubled sheet of paper taking a layer across either side of the spine to form a cap.

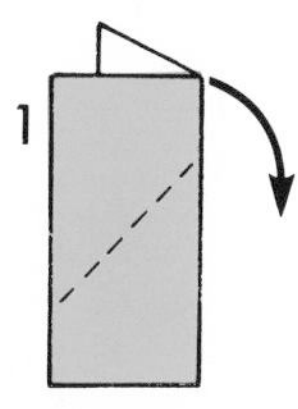

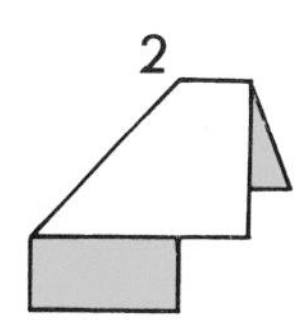

Squash fold Swivel the upper layer only of a doubled sheet of paper.

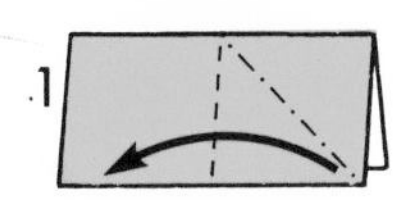

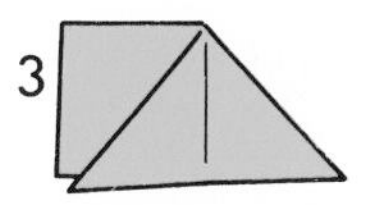

Crimp Swivel the upper layer of a doubled sheet of paper and repeat behind.

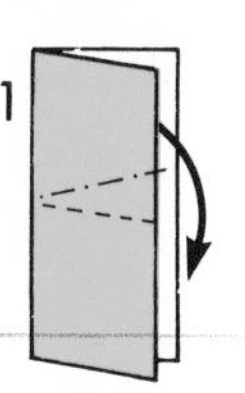

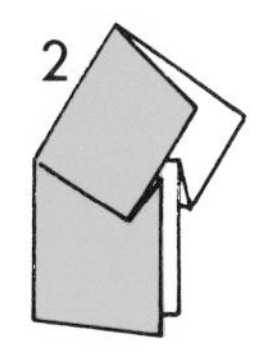

Rabbit-ear fold A method of raising a point from a triangular flap; fig. 1 shows the notation when this fold is used in the instructions for a particular model. 2) Fold two edges together and return. 3) Fold another two edges together and return. 4) Fold the remaining pair of edges together and . . . 5) . . . finally bring all three edges together. 6) The completed rabbit-ear fold.

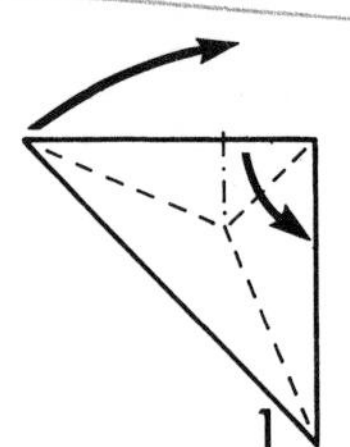

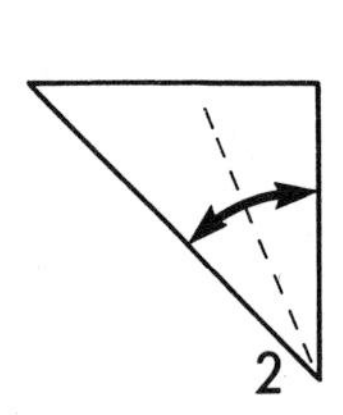

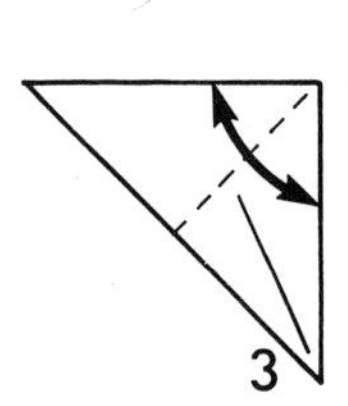

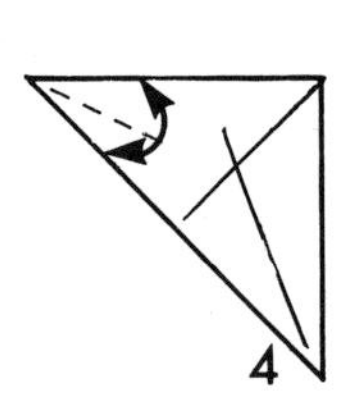

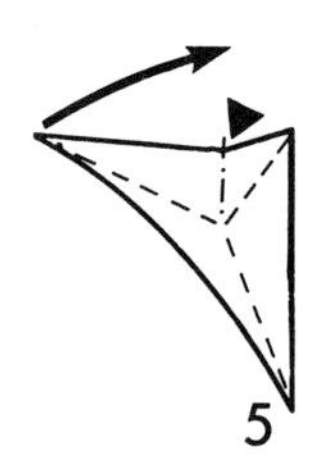

Sink A method of pushing in a point or edge between four layers of paper; fig. 1 shows the notation used in the diagrams. Mark the crease line and open up the paper. 2) Make the square of crease lines into mountain folds; push in the centre and flatten. 3) The completed sink.

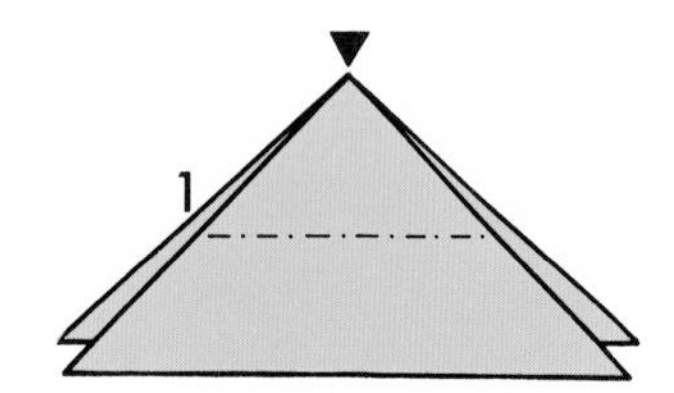

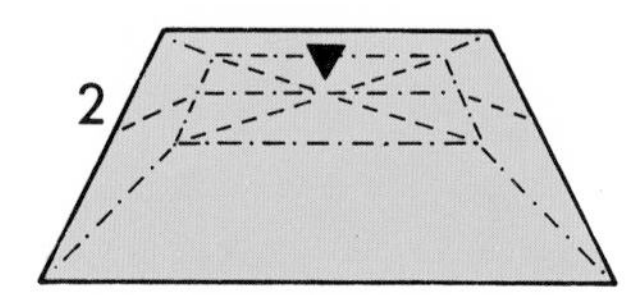

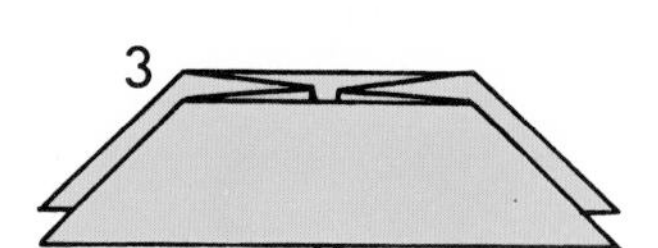

Double sink Fig. 1 shows the notation used in the diagrams. Mark the crease lines and open up the paper. 2) Make the two squares of crease lines into mountain folds and valley folds respectively; push in and reflatten. 3) The completed double sink.

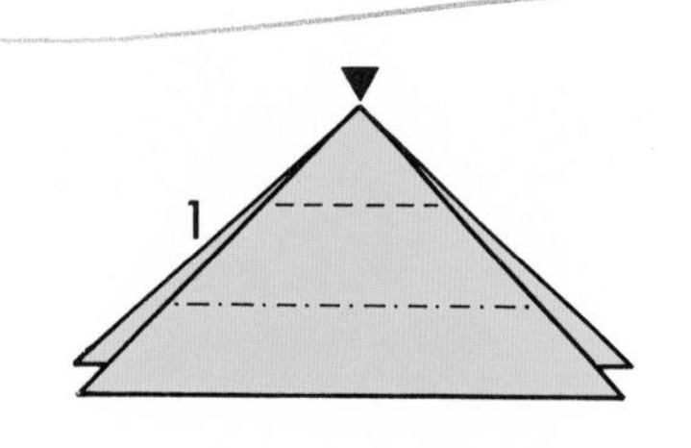

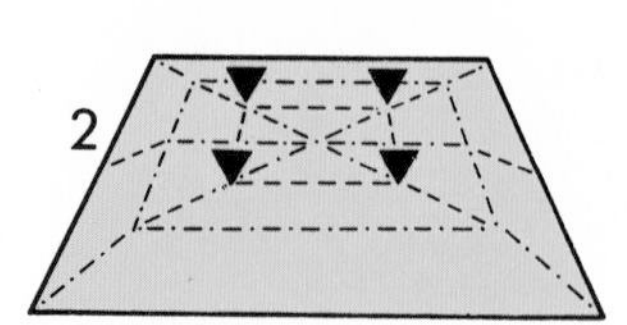

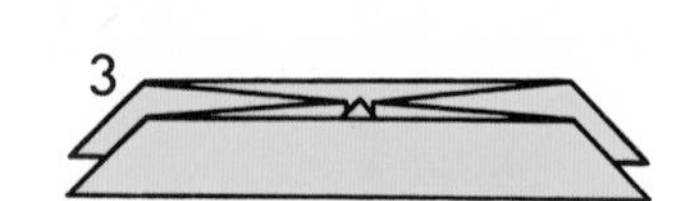

Petal fold Fig 1 shows the notation used in the diagrams. 2) Fold the raw edges to the vertical centre line. 3) Fold the top point down over the horizontal edges and return. 4) Now raise the bottom point allowing the side points to come together . . . 5) . . . like this. 6) The completed petal fold.

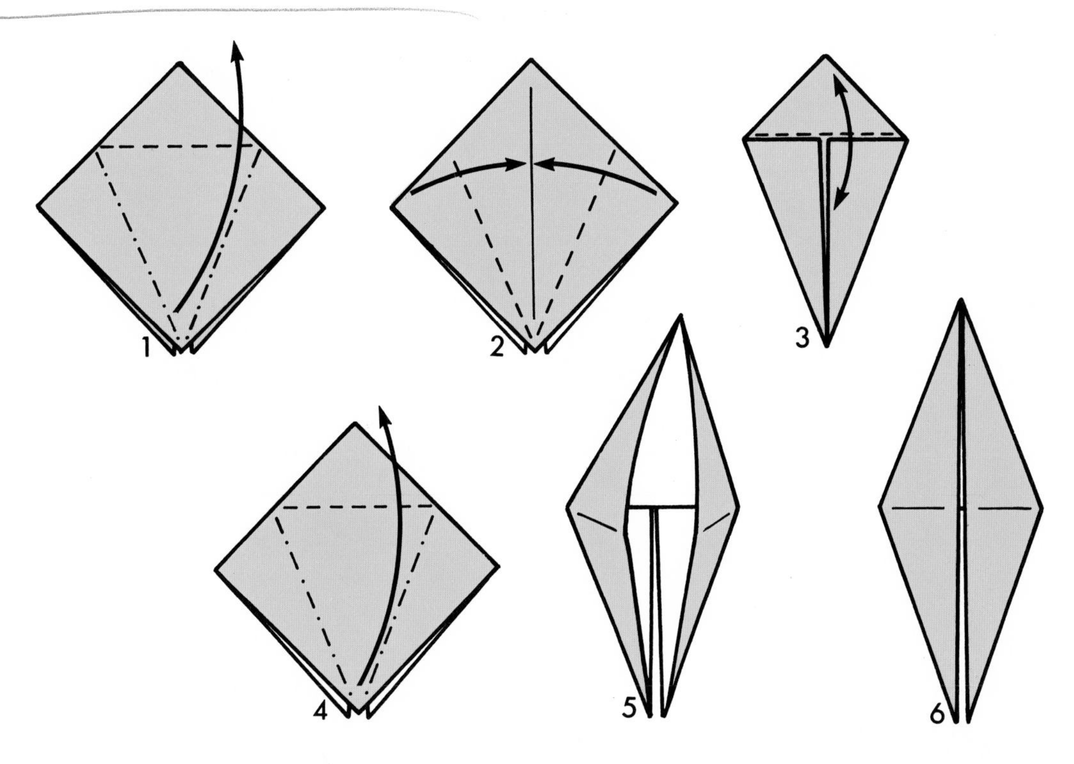

Repeat on remaining three sides/flaps This phrase occurs only when there are four flaps clustered around a central axis. First complete the procedure indicated in fig. 1 (in this case a squash fold), then turn the paper over and repeat the procedure on the reverse side. Turn the paper back again and . . . 2) . . . take the flap across to the left. 3) Repeat step 1 on the newly exposed flap; then repeat steps 2 and 3 behind. 4) Completed.

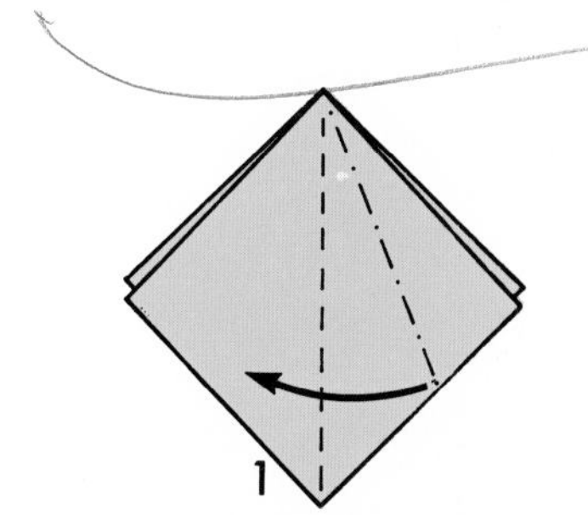

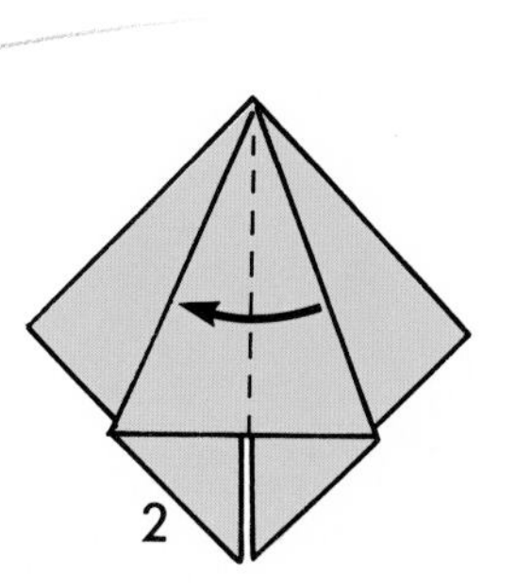

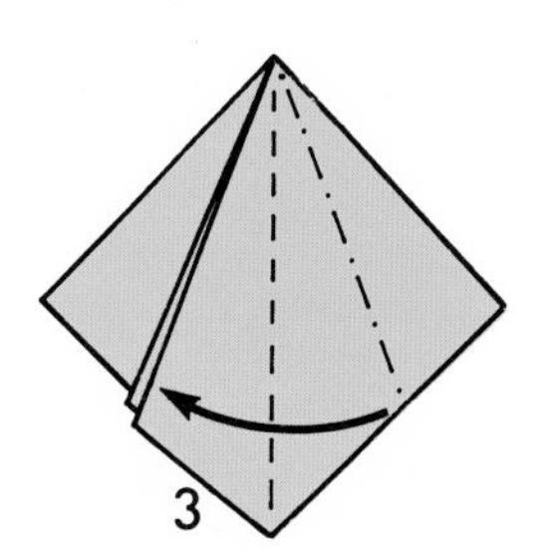

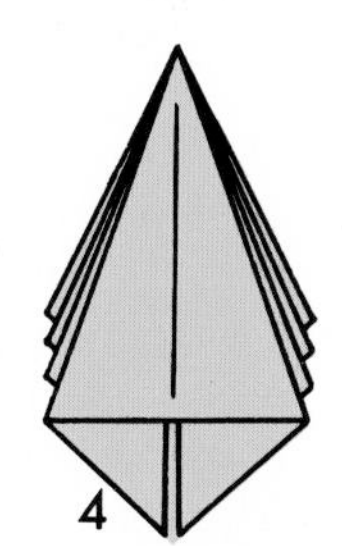

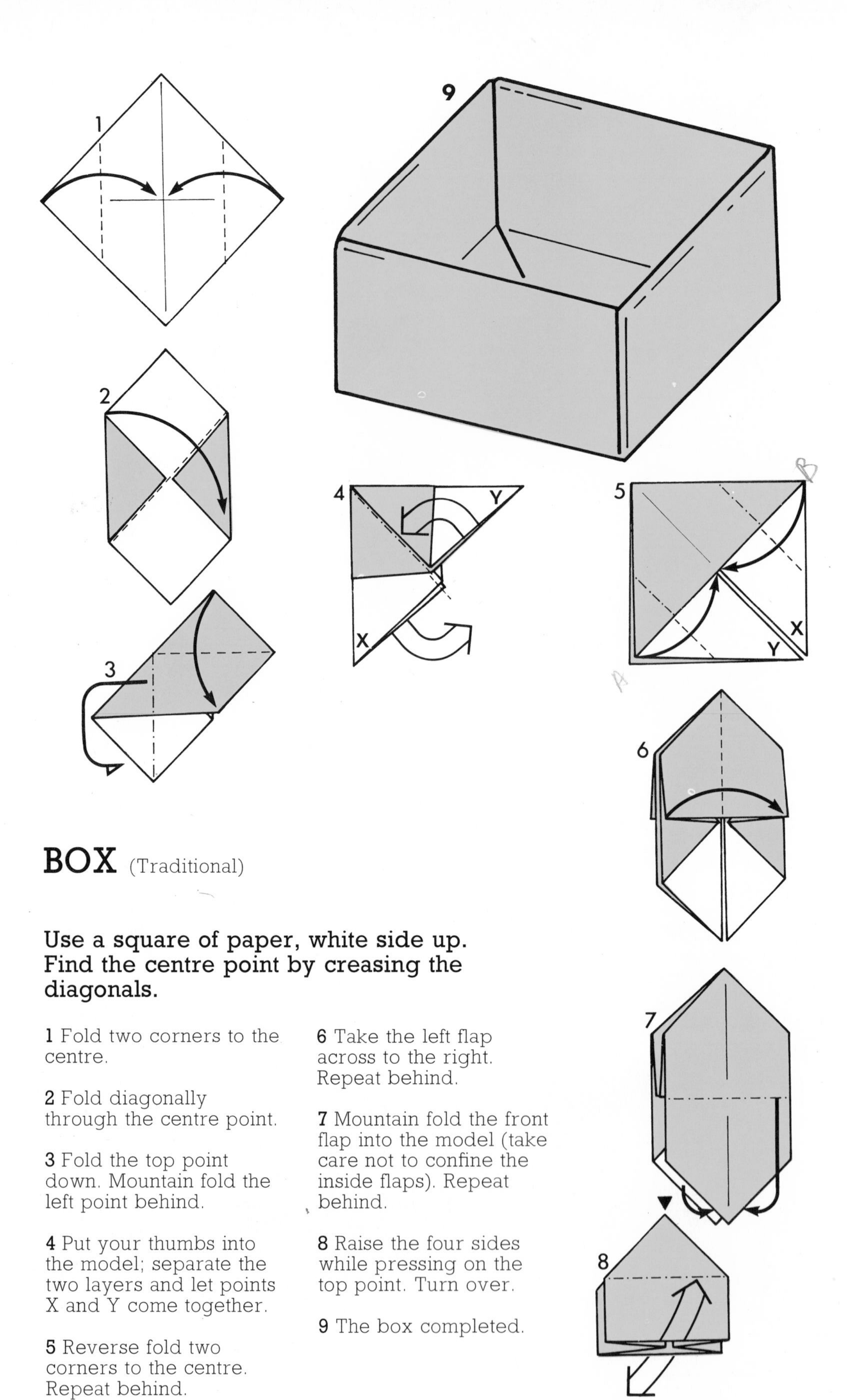

BOX (Traditional)

Use a square of paper, white side up. Find the centre point by creasing the diagonals.

1 Fold two corners to the centre.

2 Fold diagonally through the centre point.

3 Fold the top point down. Mountain fold the left point behind.

4 Put your thumbs into the model; separate the two layers and let points X and Y come together.

5 Reverse fold two corners to the centre. Repeat behind.

6 Take the left flap across to the right. Repeat behind.

7 Mountain fold the front flap into the model (take care not to confine the inside flaps). Repeat behind.

8 Raise the four sides while pressing on the top point. Turn over.

9 The box completed.

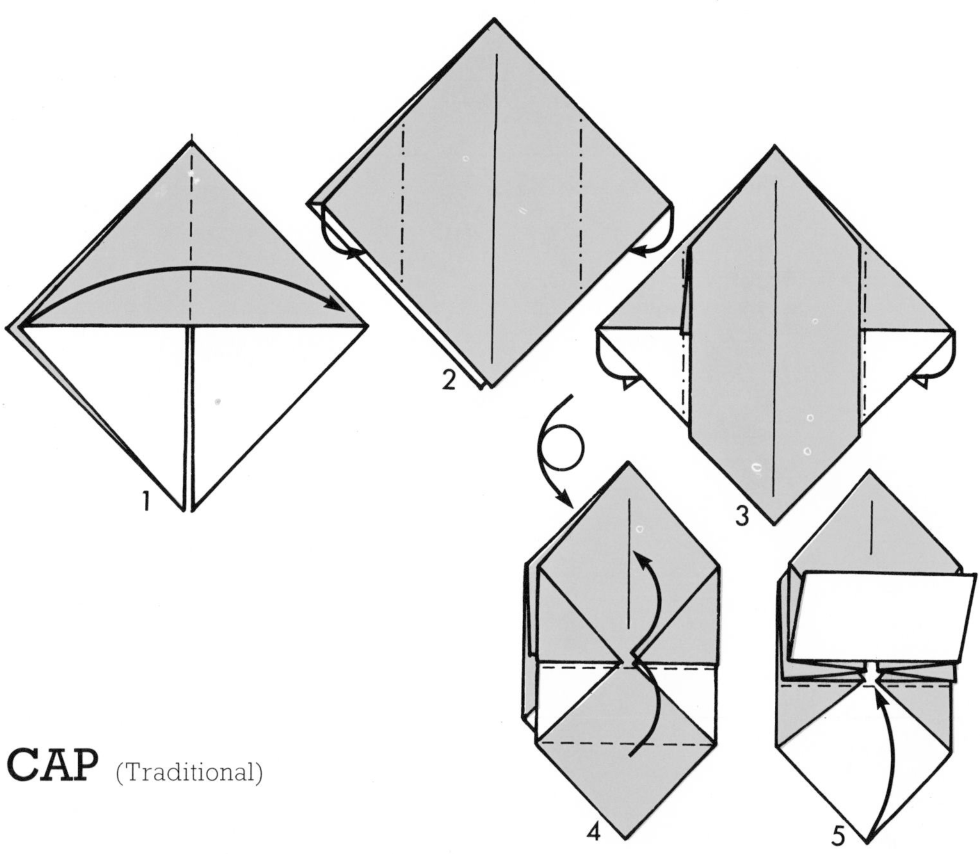

CAP (Traditional)

Use a square of paper, white side up. To make a wearable cap you need to use paper about 40 cm (16 in) square. Complete steps 1–5 of the box on page 14 and then continue as follows:

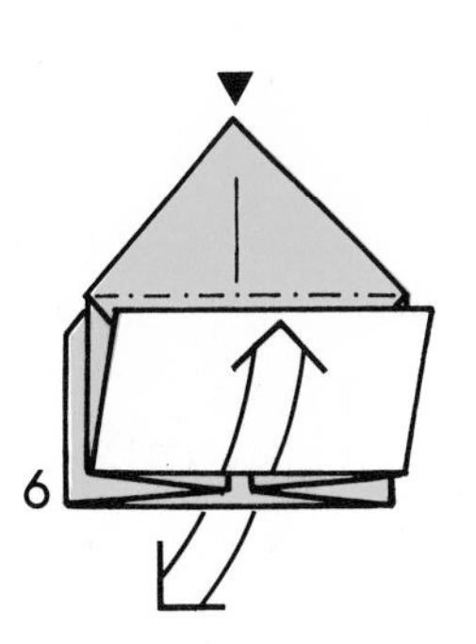

1 Take the left flap across to the right. Repeat behind.

2 Reverse fold left and right corners to the centre.

3 Mountain fold remaining left and right corners to the centre behind. Turn over.

3 Fold bottom point to the centre; then fold up again.

5 Fold remaining bottom point into the model.

6 Raise the four sides, pressing down on the top point.

7 The cap completed.

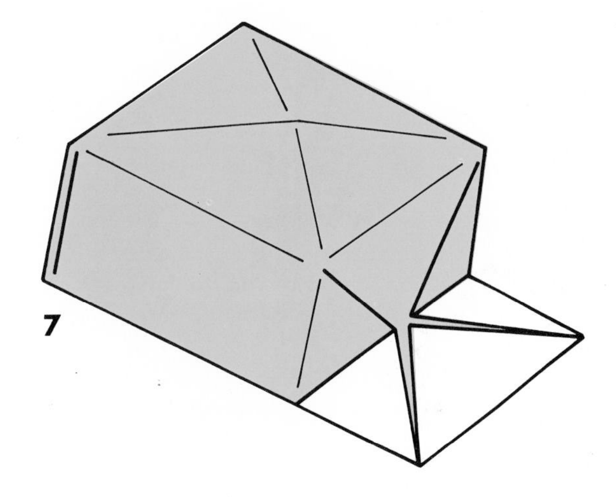

BOOK (Martin Wall)

Use a square of paper, coloured side up. You need to use paper at least 30 cm (12 in) square to make a book large enough to contain a short greeting. Complete the cap on page 15 and then continue as follows:

1 Raise the peak of the cap and bring the point to the centre of the crown.

2 Sink . . .

3 . . . like this.

4 Fold right flaps to left, in front and behind.

5 Press firmly to complete the book.

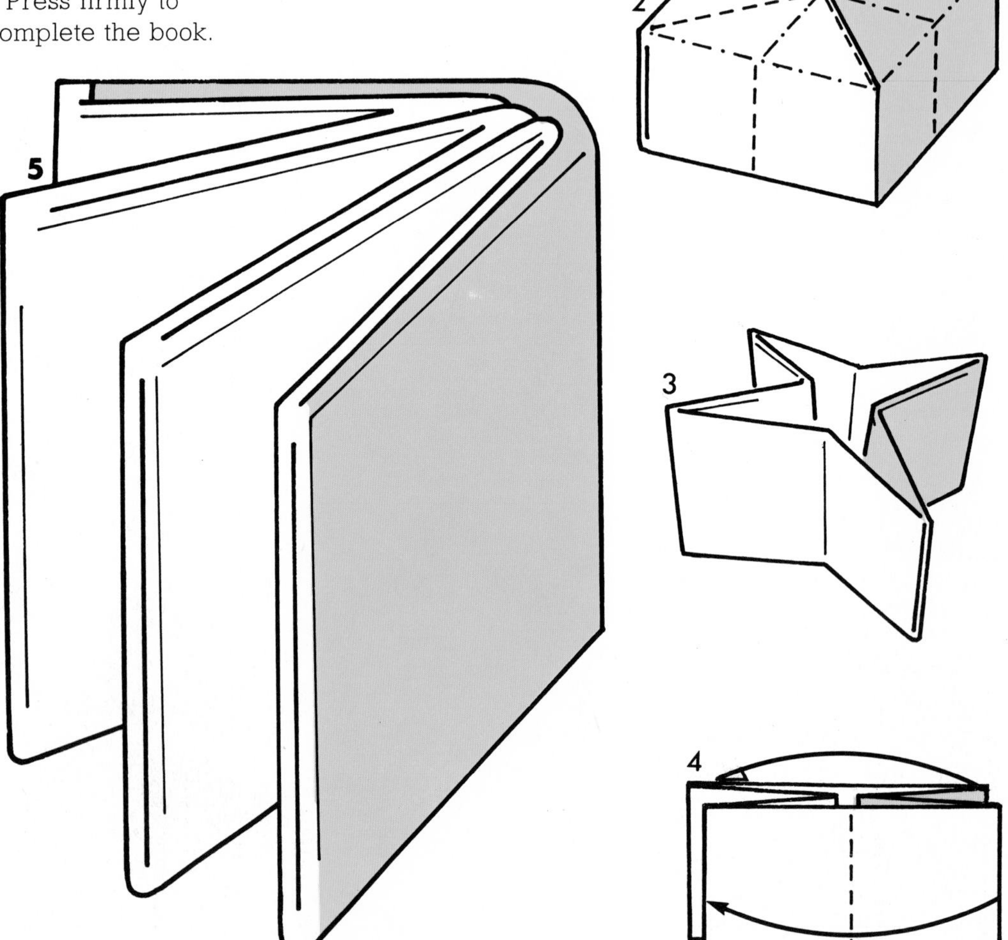

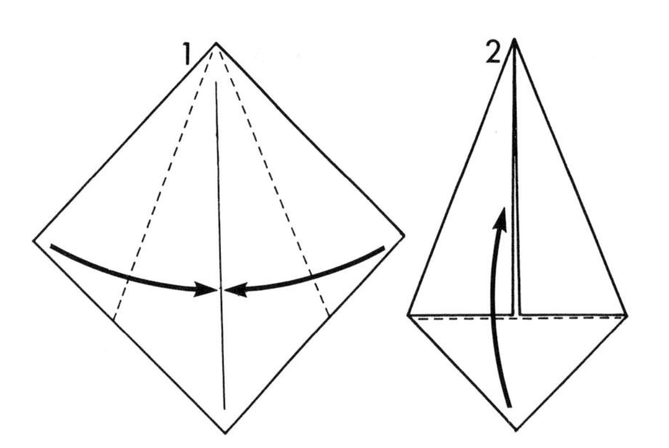

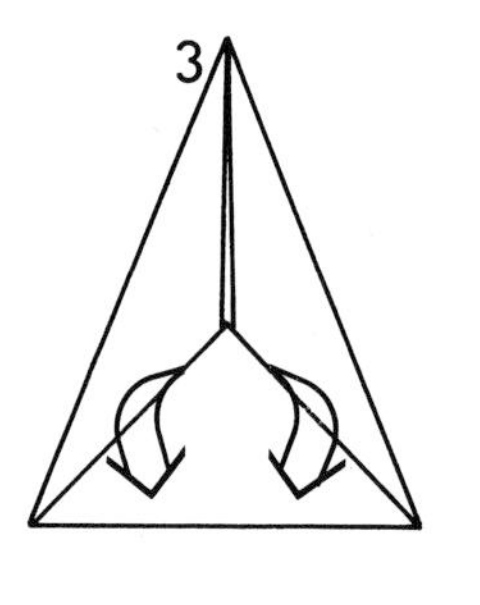

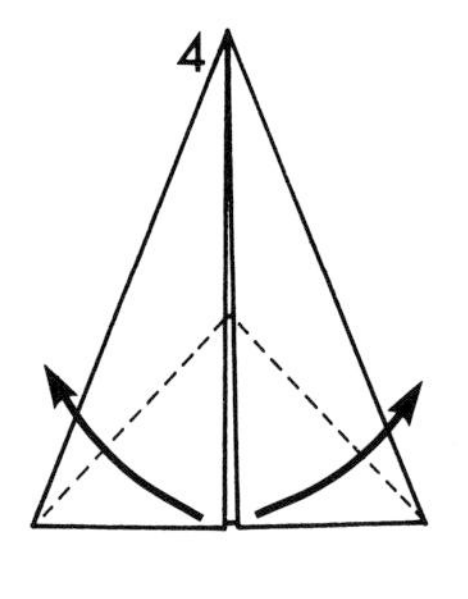

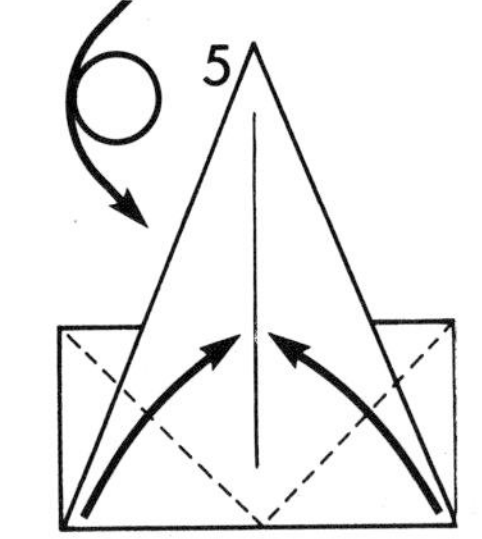

HORSE (Paul Jackson)

Use a square of white paper. Fold two corners together to mark the centre line; then open.

1 Fold the two upper sides to the centre line.

2 Fold up the triangular flap.

3 Bring the concealed flaps to the front.

4 Fold up these two flaps (fold lines run along the sides of the concealed triangular flap). Then turn over.

5 Fold bottom corners to the centre line.

6 Fold the top flap down.

7 Fold the bottom point over and over. Then turn the paper over.

8 Fold the model in half; at the same time, pull forward and collapse the middle flap.

9 Outside reverse fold to form horse's neck.

10 Inside reverse fold at top to form horse's head. Form tail at bottom.

11 The horse completed.

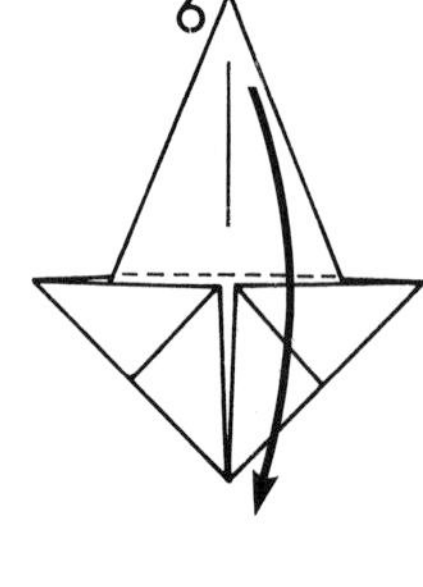

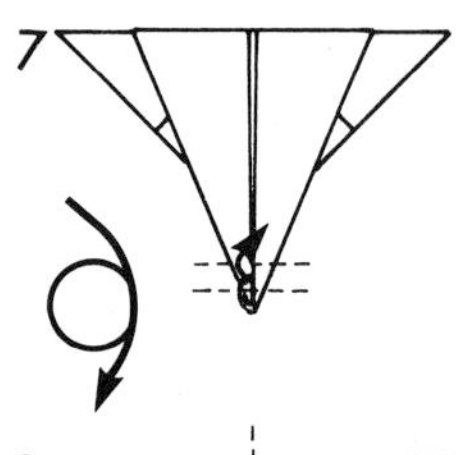

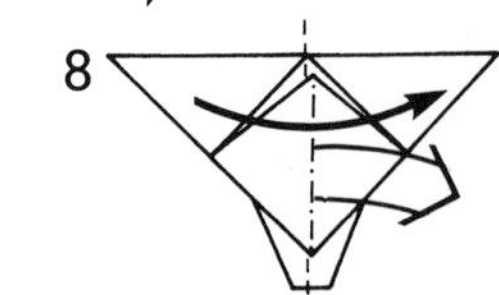

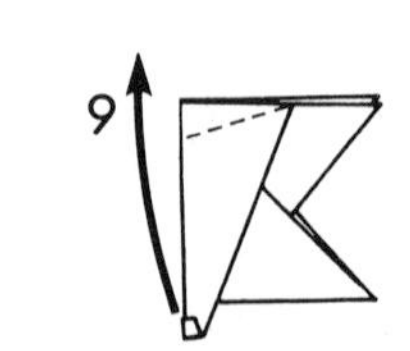

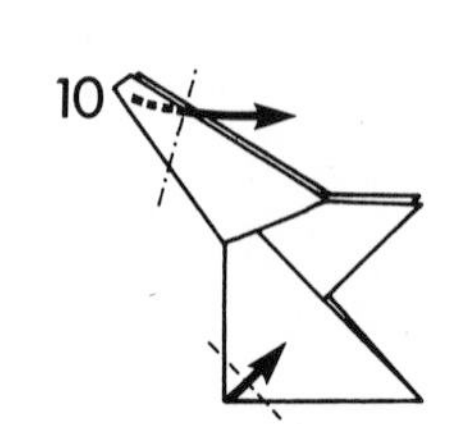

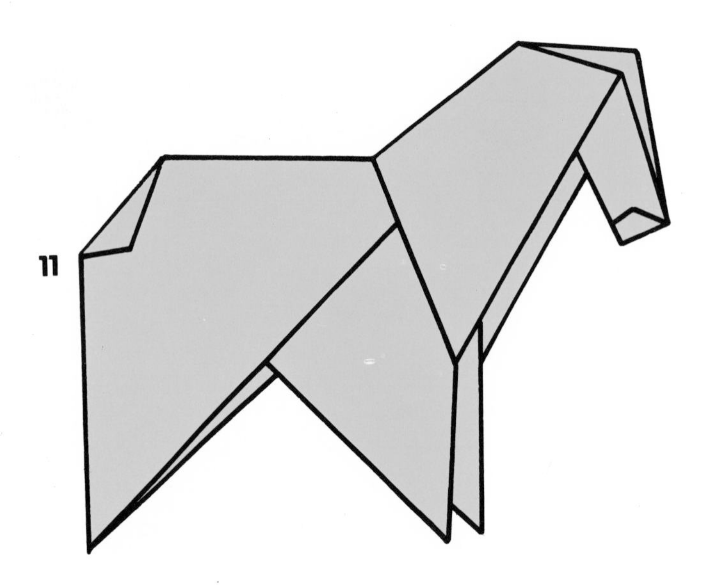

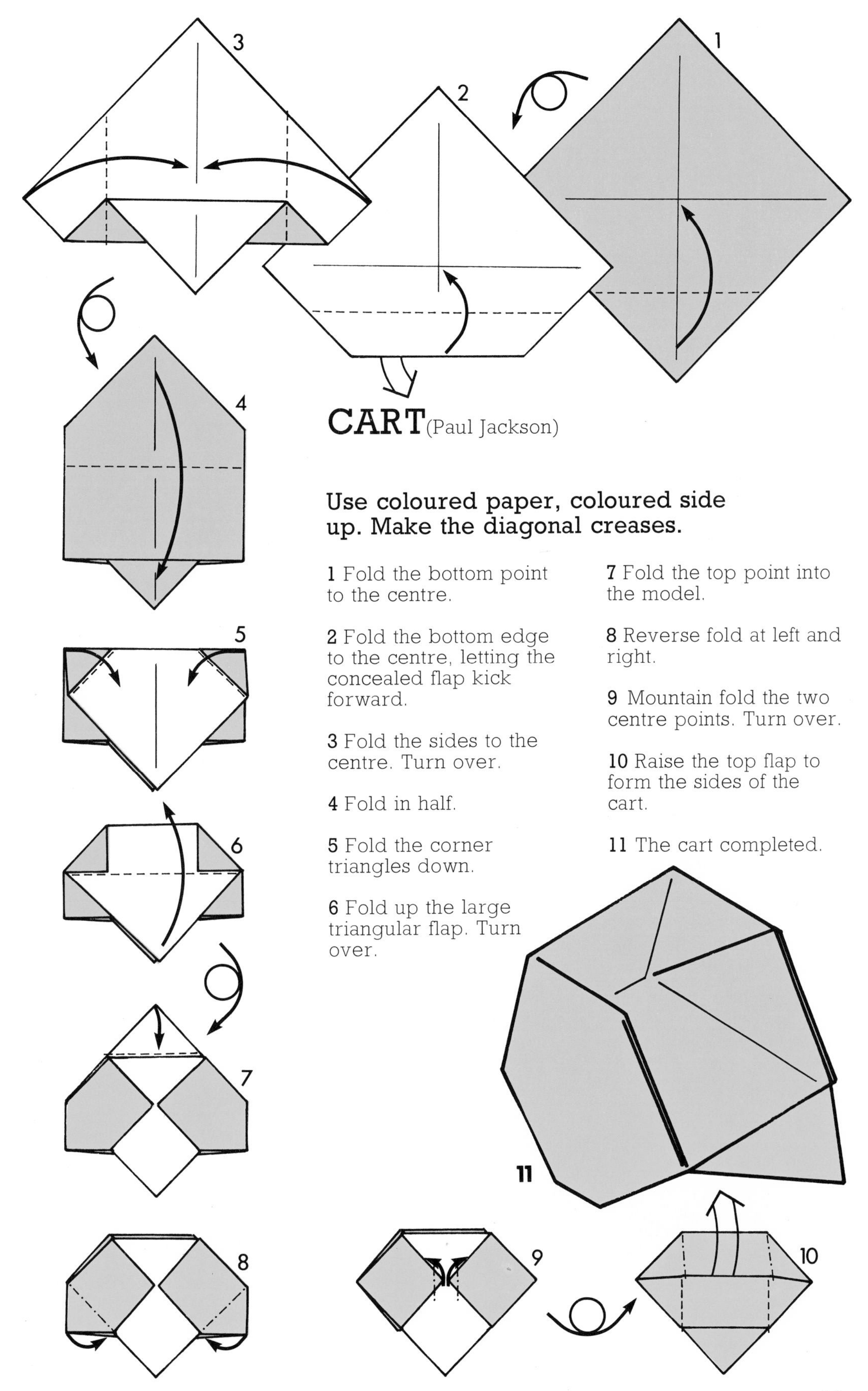

CART (Paul Jackson)

Use coloured paper, coloured side up. Make the diagonal creases.

1 Fold the bottom point to the centre.

2 Fold the bottom edge to the centre, letting the concealed flap kick forward.

3 Fold the sides to the centre. Turn over.

4 Fold in half.

5 Fold the corner triangles down.

6 Fold up the large triangular flap. Turn over.

7 Fold the top point into the model.

8 Reverse fold at left and right.

9 Mountain fold the two centre points. Turn over.

10 Raise the top flap to form the sides of the cart.

11 The cart completed.

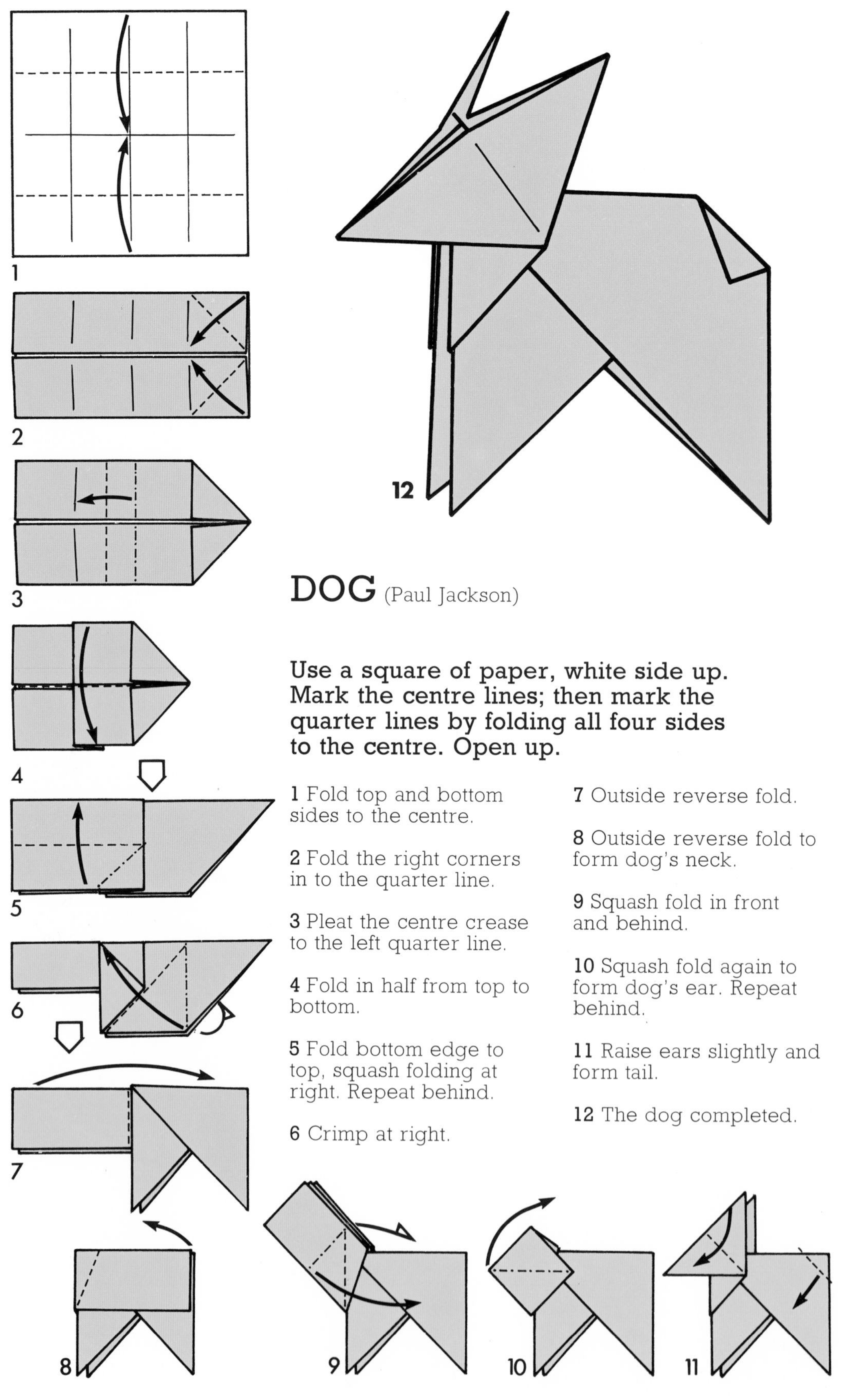

DOG (Paul Jackson)

Use a square of paper, white side up. Mark the centre lines; then mark the quarter lines by folding all four sides to the centre. Open up.

1 Fold top and bottom sides to the centre.

2 Fold the right corners in to the quarter line.

3 Pleat the centre crease to the left quarter line.

4 Fold in half from top to bottom.

5 Fold bottom edge to top, squash folding at right. Repeat behind.

6 Crimp at right.

7 Outside reverse fold.

8 Outside reverse fold to form dog's neck.

9 Squash fold in front and behind.

10 Squash fold again to form dog's ear. Repeat behind.

11 Raise ears slightly and form tail.

12 The dog completed.

FLOWER VASE (Saburo Kase)

Use a square of paper, white side up. Make the vertical centre crease.

1 Fold bottom to top.

2 Fold the bottom left corner to top centre. Mountain fold the bottom right corner to top centre behind.

3 Place the tips of your forefingers inside the model and separate the layers, allowing the side points to come together at the top.

4 Fold left and right corners to the centre line and return. Repeat behind.

5 Reverse fold, using the crease lines just made. Repeat behind.

6 Mountain fold the top point into the model, covering the small inner flap at right . . .

7 . . . like this (a view of the reverse side of the upper layers). Repeat behind.

8 Fold right flap to left. Repeat behind.

9 Repeat step 6.

10 Fold the top corners and return. Repeat behind.

11 Reverse fold, using these crease lines. Repeat behind.

12 Flatten the bottom point; place a finger inside the model at top and raise the four sides of the vase.

13 The vase completed. Its shape can be altered by altering the position of the crease lines in step 4.

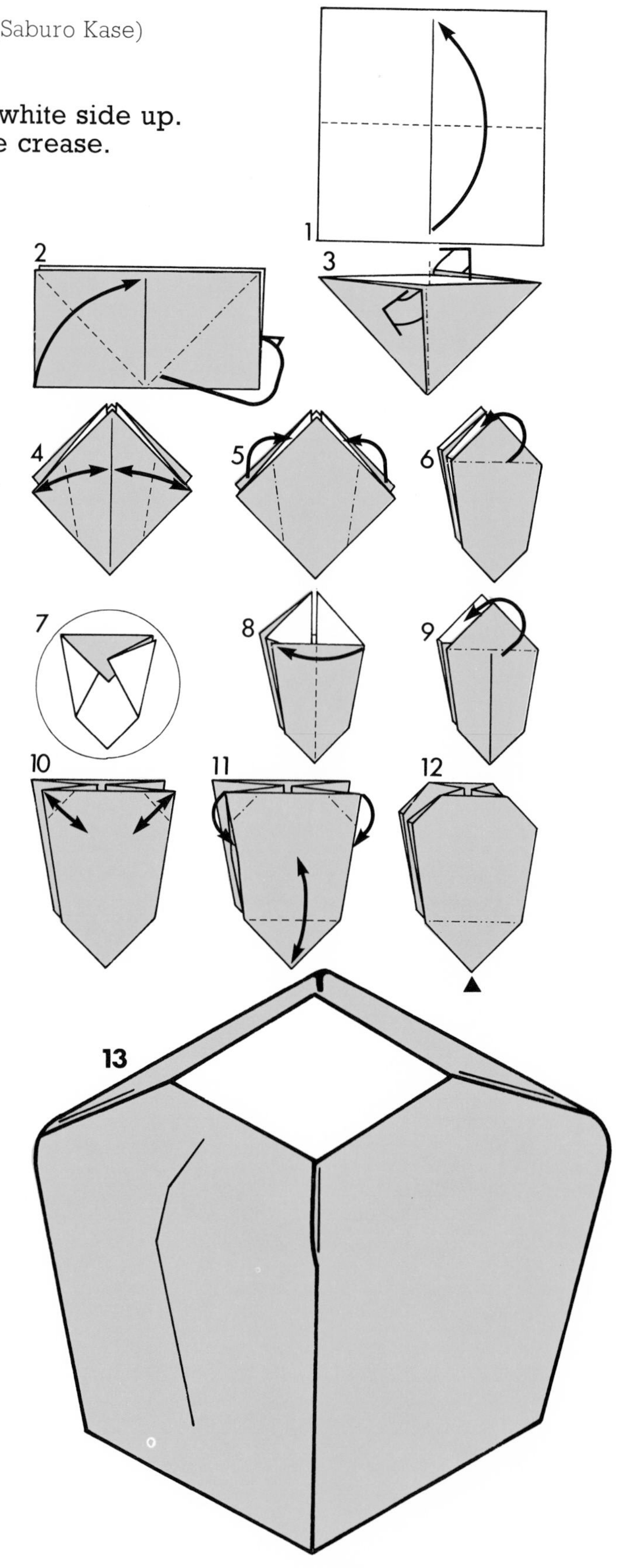

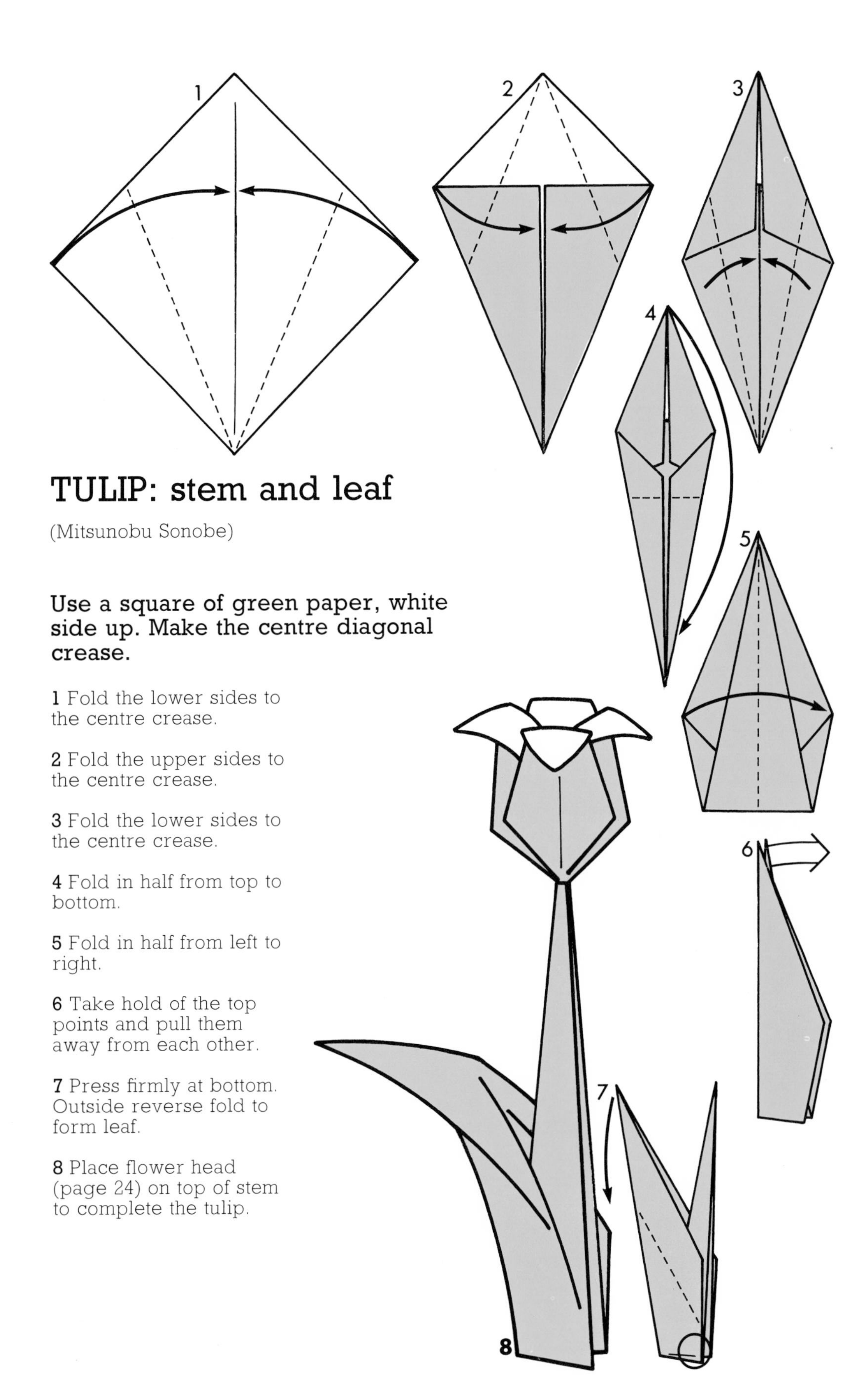

TULIP: stem and leaf

(Mitsunobu Sonobe)

Use a square of green paper, white side up. Make the centre diagonal crease.

1 Fold the lower sides to the centre crease.

2 Fold the upper sides to the centre crease.

3 Fold the lower sides to the centre crease.

4 Fold in half from top to bottom.

5 Fold in half from left to right.

6 Take hold of the top points and pull them away from each other.

7 Press firmly at bottom. Outside reverse fold to form leaf.

8 Place flower head (page 24) on top of stem to complete the tulip.

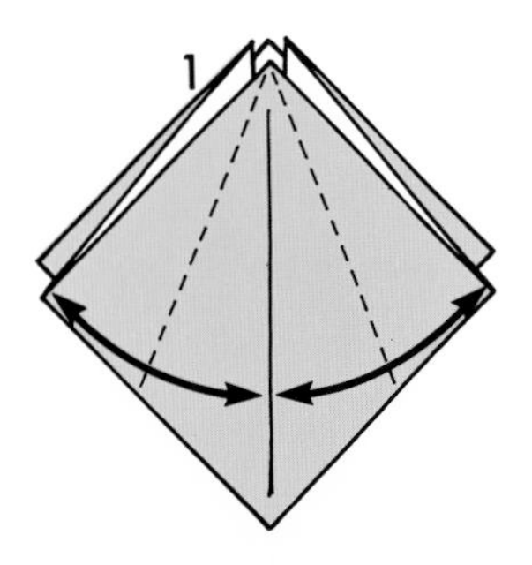

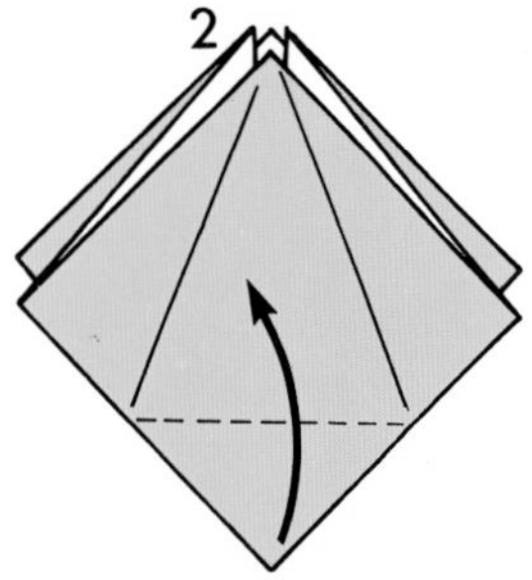

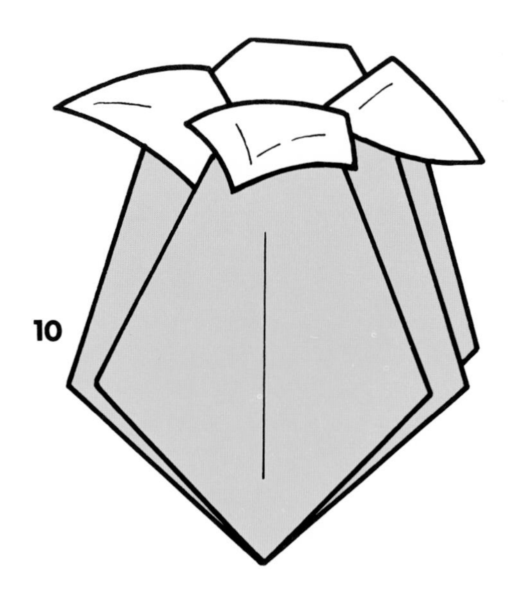

TULIP: flower (Mitsunobu Sonobe)

Use a square of coloured paper. The length of each side should be about two-thirds of the length of each side of the square used for the stem and leaf (page 23). Complete steps 1–3 of the vase on page 22 and then continue as follows:

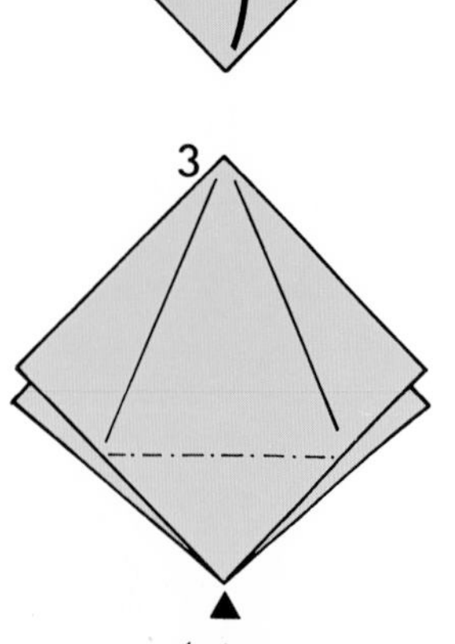

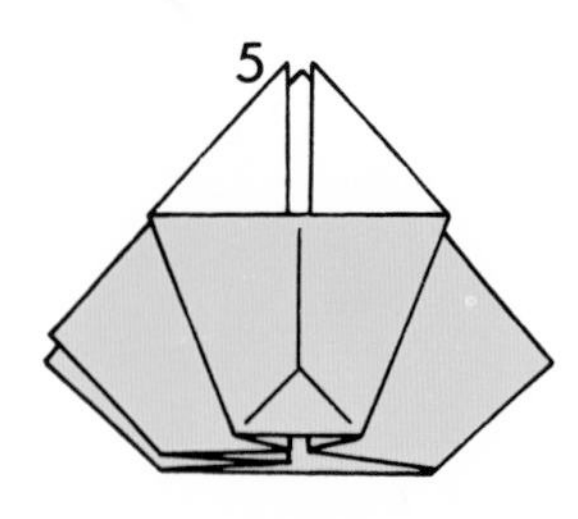

1 Fold the upper edges to the centre line, crease and return.

2 Fold the bottom point up, crease and return.

3 Sink, using the crease line just made.

4 Squash right flap; at the same time, press and flatten the concealed, inside flap at bottom.

5 This is the result. Repeat on remaining three flaps.

6 Petal fold. Repeat on other three sides.

7 Fold corners up over folded edge. Repeat on other three sides.

8 Fold right flap to left. Repeat behind.

9 Turn the four top points inside out. Place a finger inside to open out the flower.

10 The tulip flower completed. Place on stem (page 23).

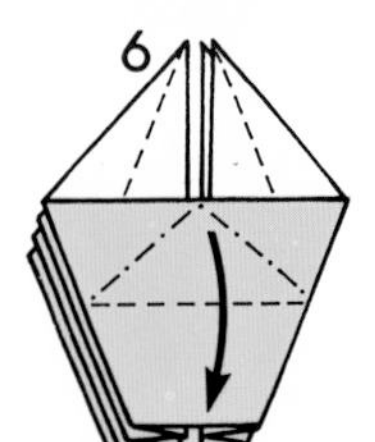

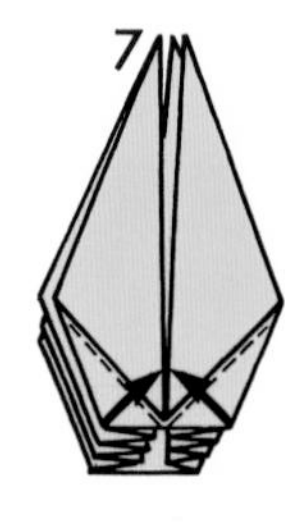

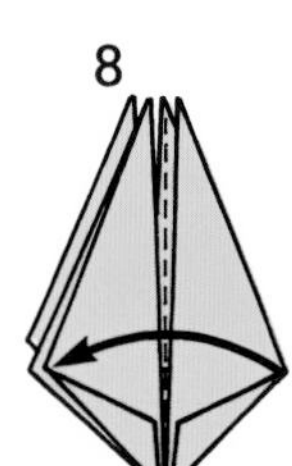

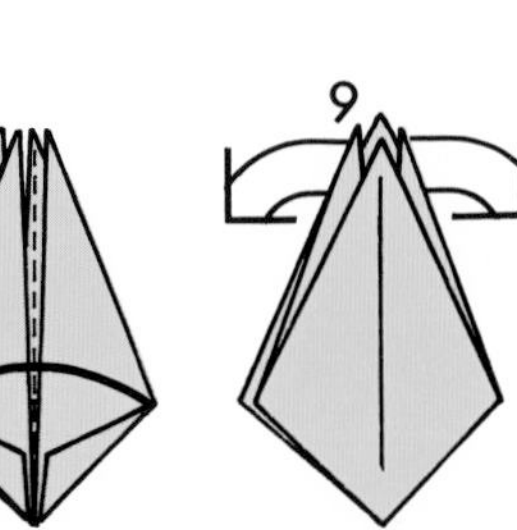

CHRISTMAS TREE

(Makoto Yamaguchi)

Prepare about eight squares of green paper, slightly decreasing in size, to make the foliage. Use one square of grey or brown paper, equal in size to the largest green square, to make the trunk. To make a tree about 30 cm (12 in) high, the largest square should be about 30 cm (12 in) square, and the other squares should decrease in size by about 2.5 cm (1 in) each.

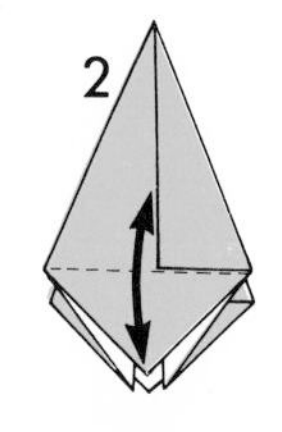

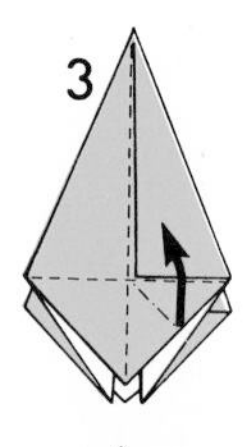

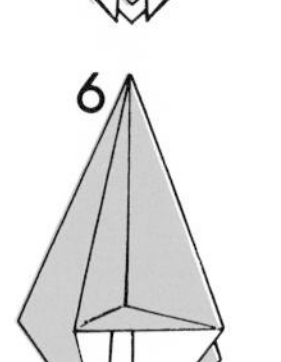

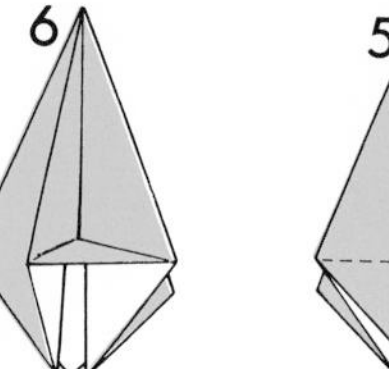

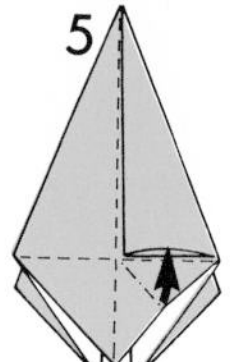

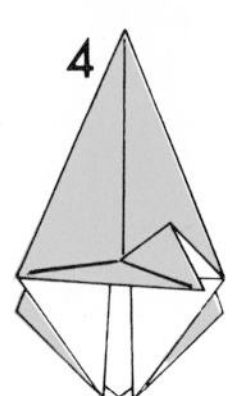

Foliage

1 Take the largest green square and complete steps 1–3 of the vase (page 22). Rotate it so that the open edges are at the bottom. Fold the bottom point to the top, crease and return. Repeat on other three sides.

2 Take the bottom point to the right.

3 Crease firmly and mountain fold the small triangular flap into the model . . .

4 . . . like this. Repeat on other three sides.

5 One unit completed. Construct the smaller units in the same way and place them one on top of another.

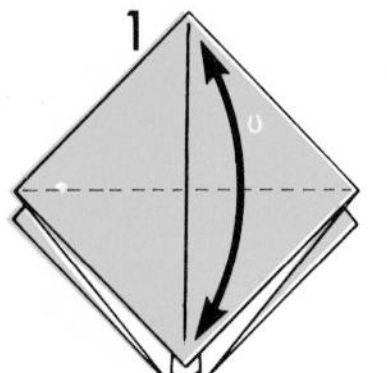

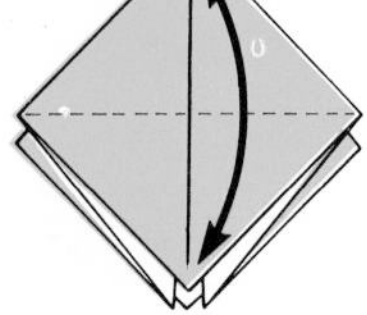

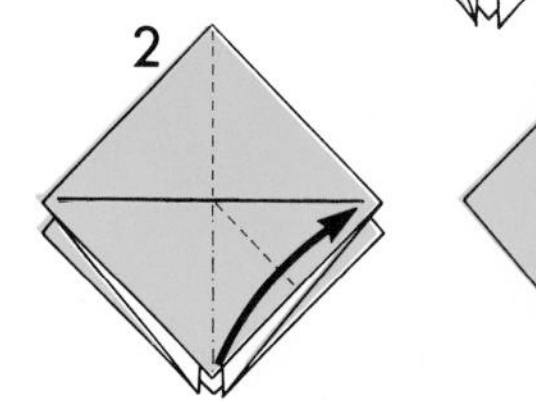

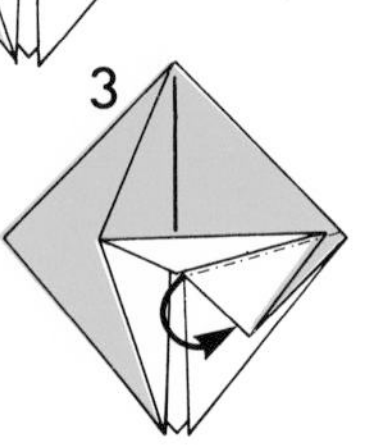

Trunk

1 Take the remaining square and complete steps 1–3 of the vase (page 22). Rotate so that the open edges are at the bottom. Fold the top right side to the centre line. Repeat on other three sides.

2 Fold the bottom point up over the horizontal edge, crease and return. Repeat on other three sides.

3 Take the bottom point to the right . . .

4 . . . like this. Crease firmly and return. Repeat on other three sides.

5 Fold the small triangular flap into the pocket . . .

6 . . . like this. Repeat on other three sides.

7 The trunk completed.

8 Place the foliage onto the trunk to complete the Christmas tree.

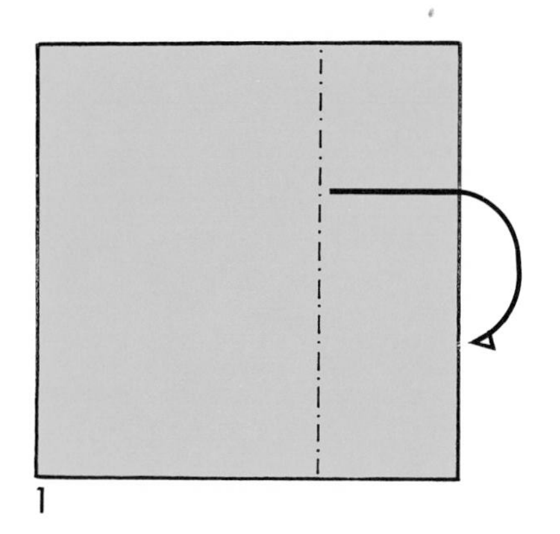

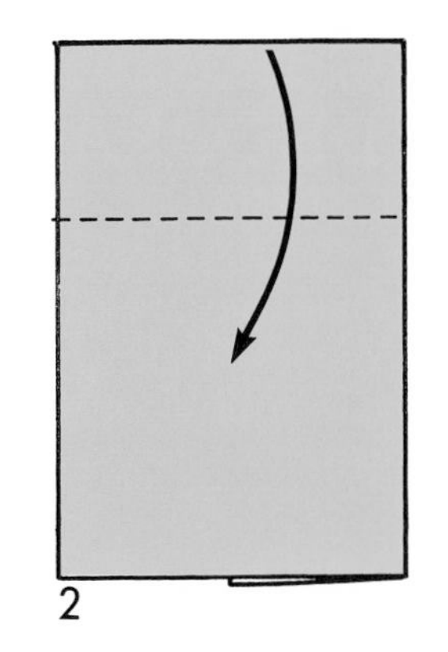

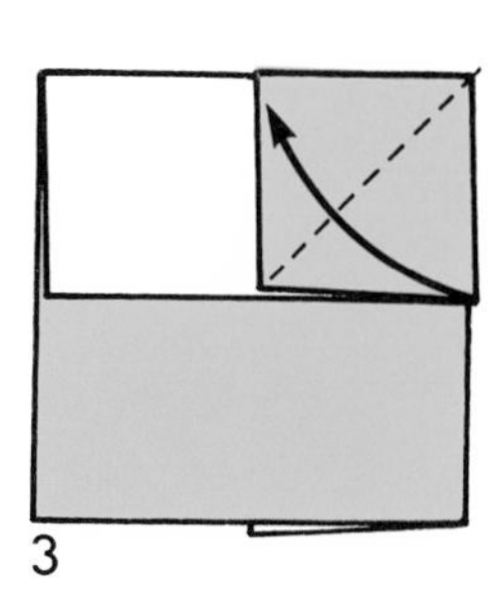

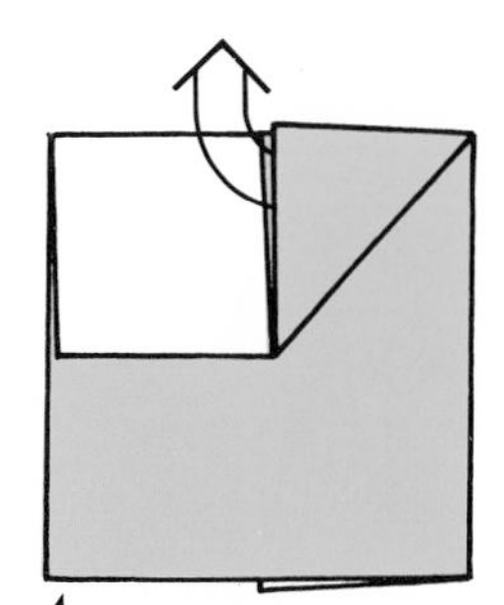

CANDLE (Yoshihide Momotani)

Use a square of red paper, coloured side up.

1 Mountain fold on a line one-third of the way from the right.

2 Fold on a line one-third of the way from the top.

3 Fold the little square diagonally in half.

4 Pull out the concealed flap.

5 Fold up the bottom edge. Pleat at top.

6 Fold the two corners at left.

7 Roll the paper from the right . . .

8 . . . like this. Bring the left edge over and tuck it into the pocket.

9 The candle completed. Use it to decorate your Christmas tree.

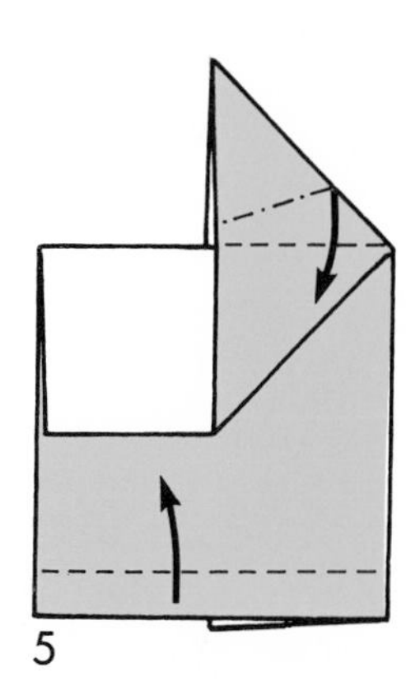

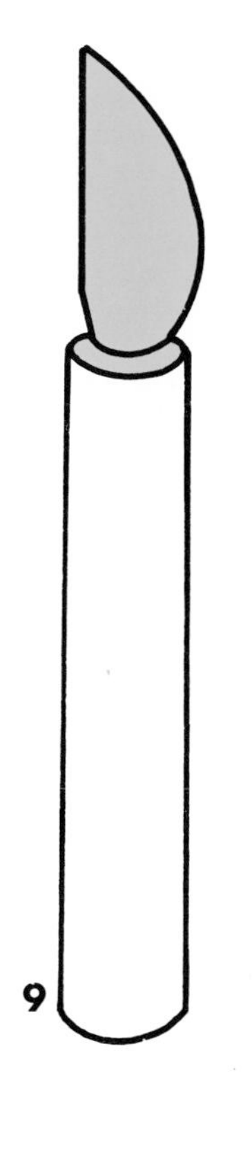

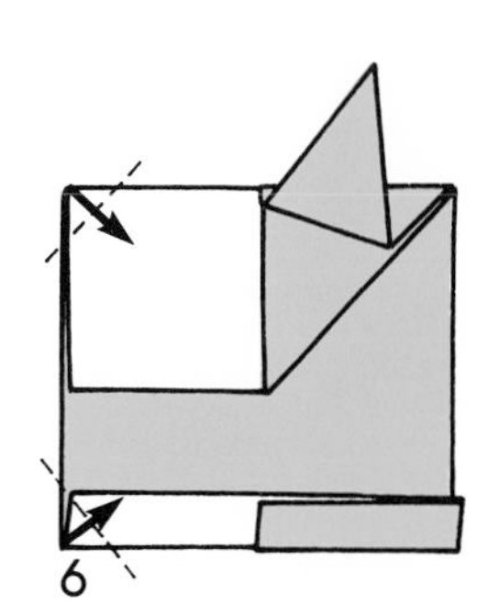

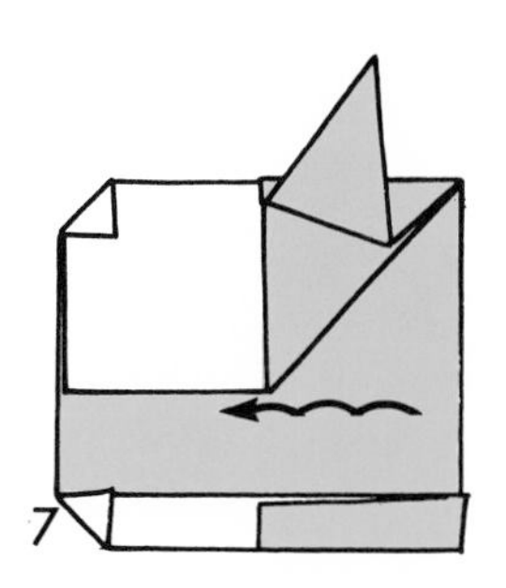

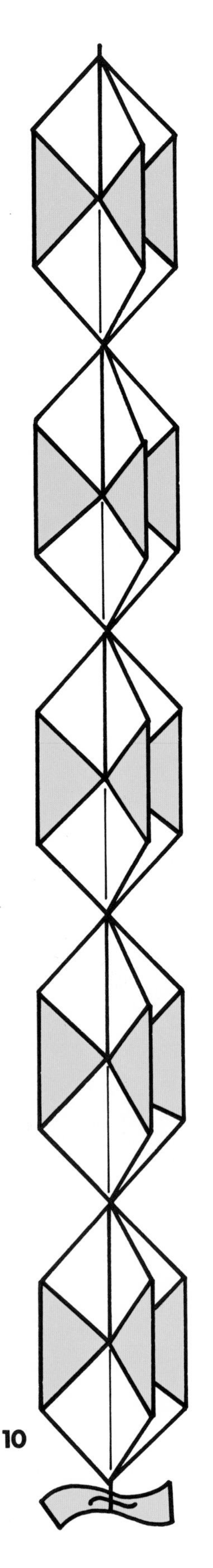

CHRISTMAS TREE DECORATION (Toshie Takahama)

Use two small squares of coloured paper, coloured side up. Crease the diagonals of each to find the centre point.

1 Take one square and fold two opposite corners to the centre. Turn over.

2 Fold the sides to the centre, allowing the flaps to kick out from underneath.

3 Mountain fold in half.

4 Fold the right flap across to the left, squashing the point at top right. Repeat behind.

5 This completes one unit. With the second square, complete steps 1–5; then fold the left flap across to the right and repeat behind.

6 This completes the second unit.

7 Fit the two units together like this. Turn over . . .

8 . . . and make sure that the point on this side is tucked into its pocket too.

9 The decoration completed.

10 You may want to thread several decorations together to make a streamer. Many streamers hung side-by-side can be used to decorate a wall.

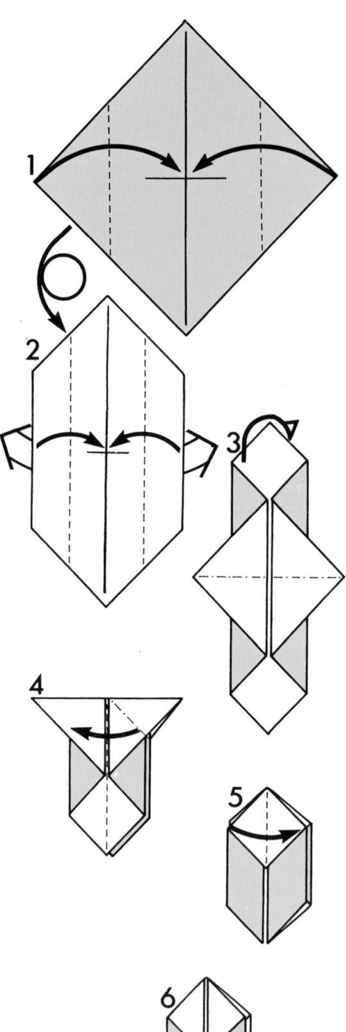

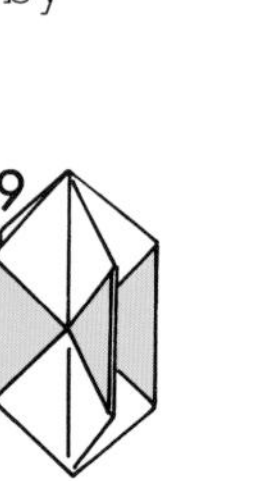

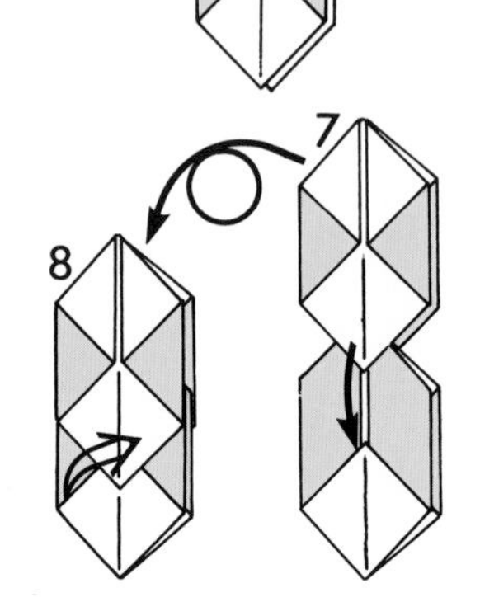

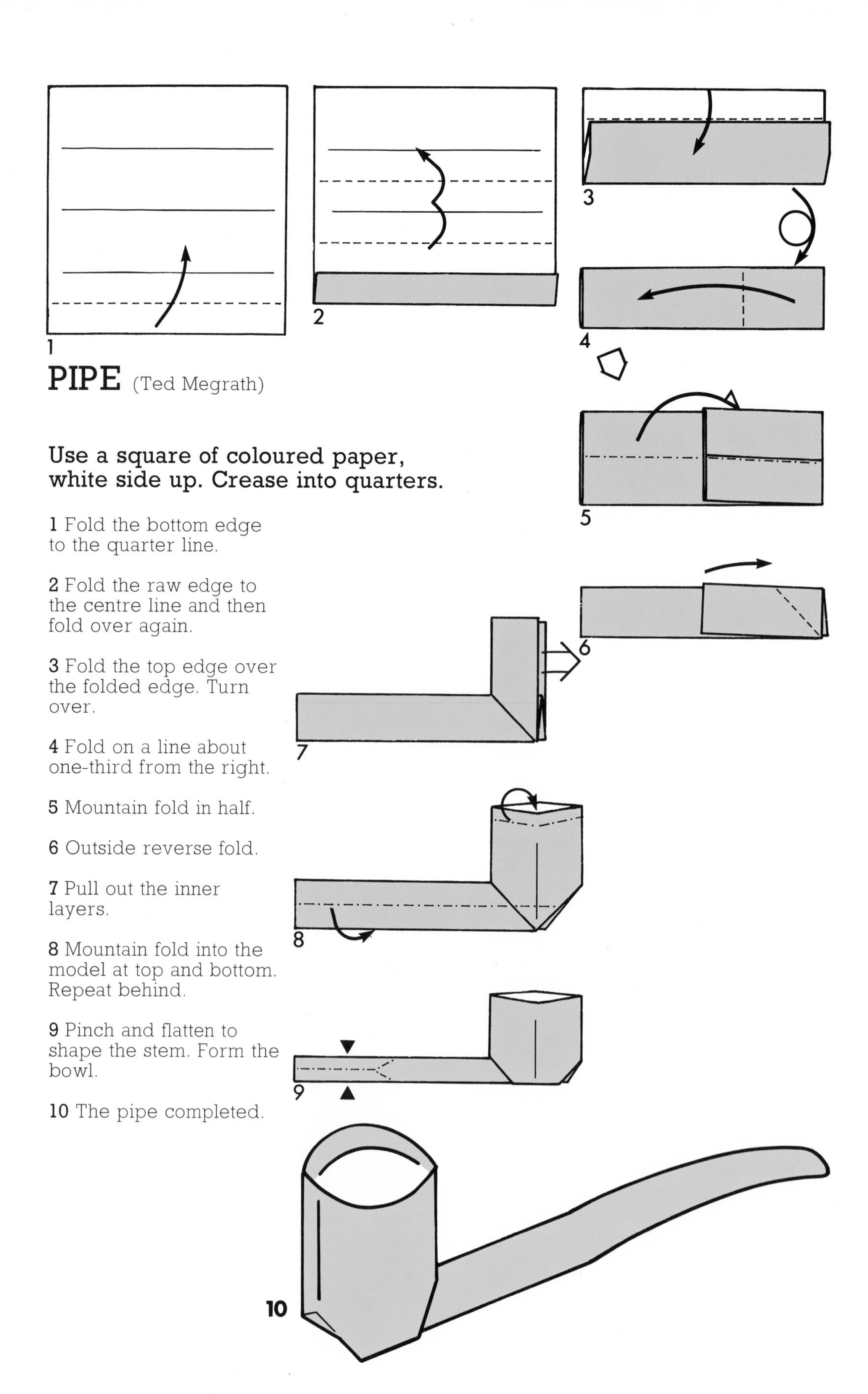

PIPE (Ted Megrath)

Use a square of coloured paper, white side up. Crease into quarters.

1 Fold the bottom edge to the quarter line.

2 Fold the raw edge to the centre line and then fold over again.

3 Fold the top edge over the folded edge. Turn over.

4 Fold on a line about one-third from the right.

5 Mountain fold in half.

6 Outside reverse fold.

7 Pull out the inner layers.

8 Mountain fold into the model at top and bottom. Repeat behind.

9 Pinch and flatten to shape the stem. Form the bowl.

10 The pipe completed.

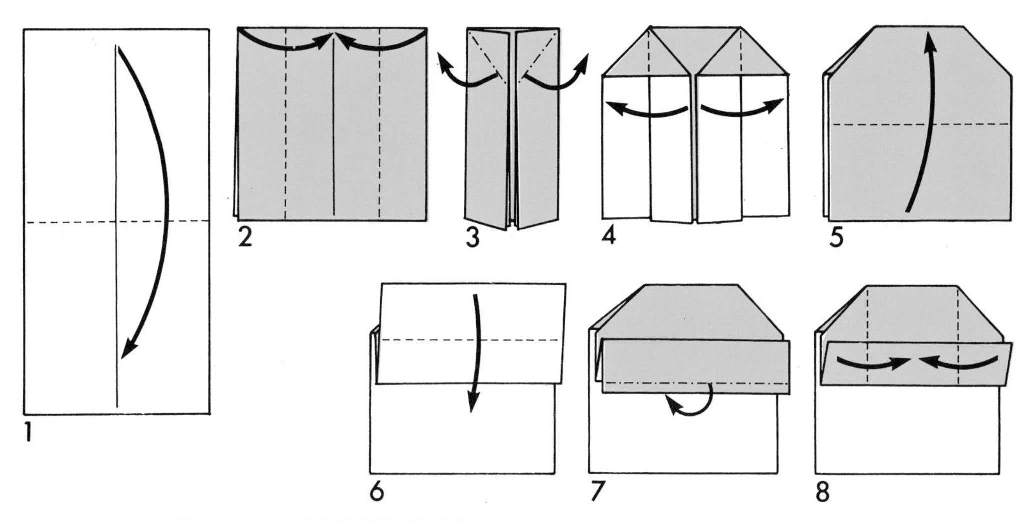

BOOK OF MATCHES (Laurie Bisman)

Use a 2 × 1 rectangle of coloured paper, white side up. Fold the two longer sides together to make the centre crease.

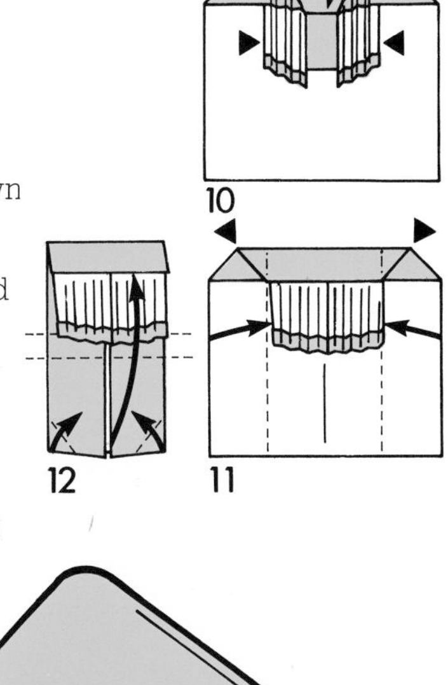

1 Fold in half.

2 Fold the sides to the centre.

3 Open the two flaps and squash.

4 Take the centre flaps to left and right.

5 Fold the bottom edge to top.

6 Fold the top edge to a point a little below the folded edge.

7 Push the raw edge up behind the concealed folded edge.

8 Fold the sides to centre.

9 Pleat the upper layer only of the centre flap.

10 Push in the sides of the centre flap to bring the centre edges together. Then fold down top edge.

11 Push in at top left and right, turning these corners inside out. Fold sides to centre.

12 Fold bottom corners; then fold the bottom edge up into the pocket at top. Rotate.

13 The book of matches completed.

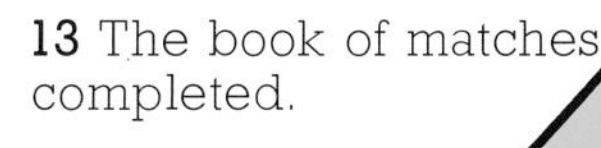

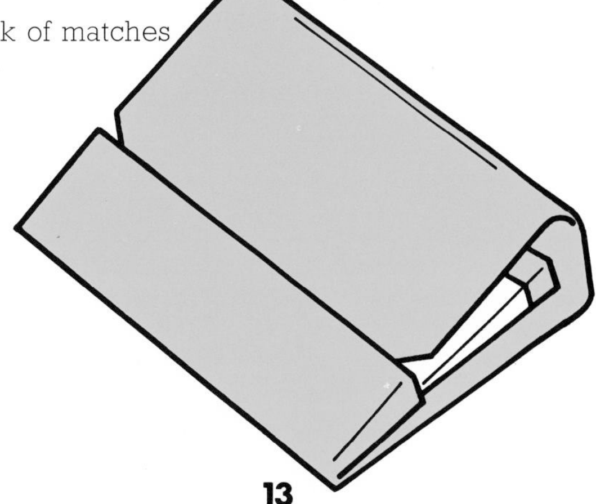

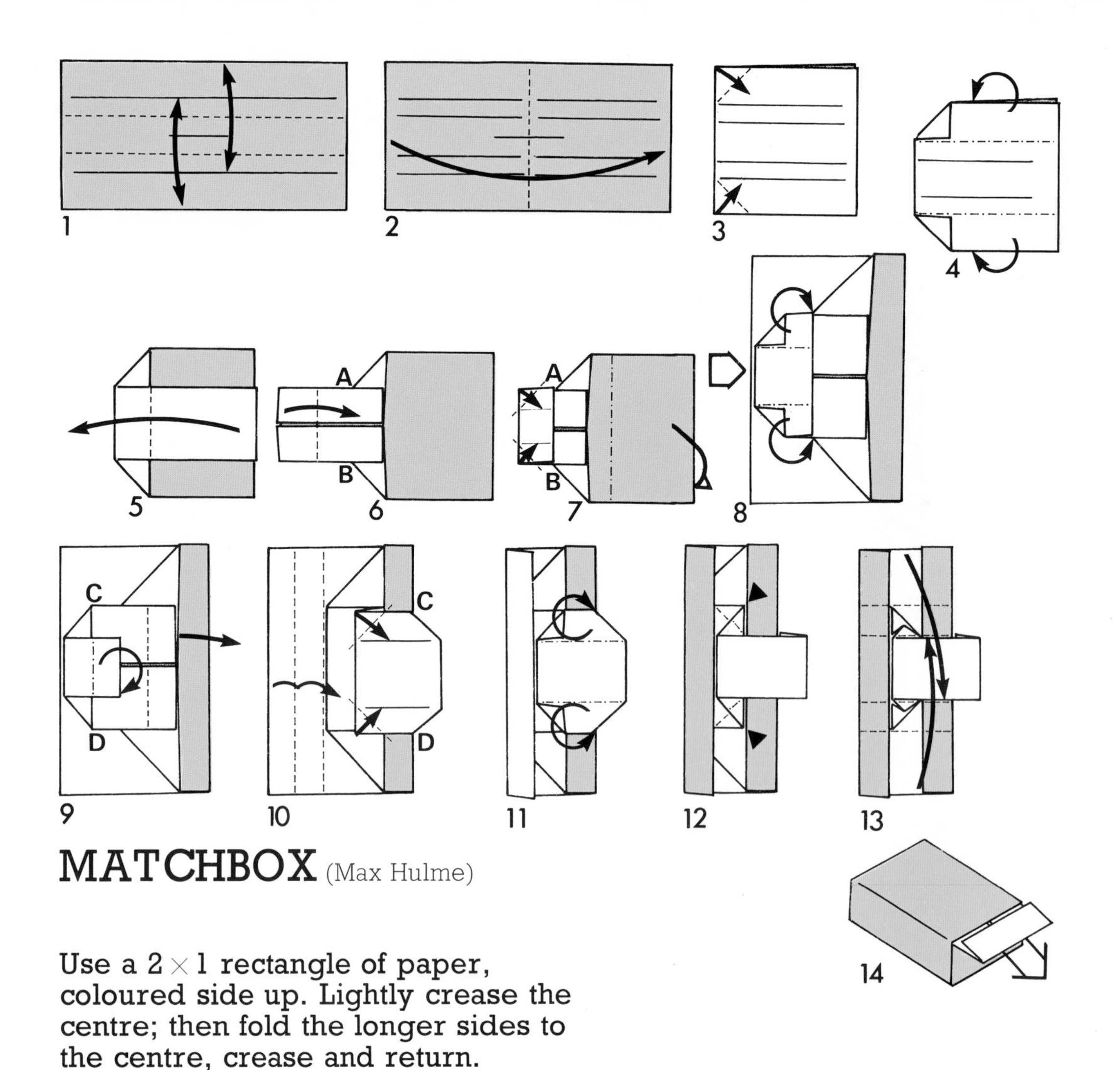

MATCHBOX (Max Hulme)

Use a 2 × 1 rectangle of paper, coloured side up. Lightly crease the centre; then fold the longer sides to the centre, crease and return.

1 Fold the longer sides in turn to the opposite quarter lines, crease and return.

2 Fold in half.

3 Fold the two corners at left to their nearest quarter lines.

4 Mountain fold at top and bottom.

5 Take the front flap to the left.

6 Fold left edge to meet angles A and B.

7 Fold two corners at left. Mountain fold in half.

8 Mountain fold at top and bottom of front flap.

9 Fold edge into pocket at left. Fold points C and D to right edge.

10 Fold left edge to folded edge and then fold over again. Fold two corners of top flap.

11 Mountain fold top and bottom of front flap.

12 Reverse folds.

13 Bring top and bottom edges together; slide one edge between the layers of the other to form box.

14 Pull flap . . .

15 . . . and the tray will pop into position. The matchbox completed.

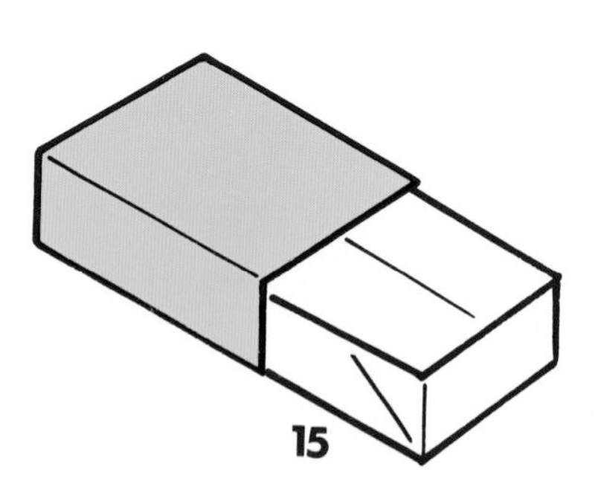

PIG (Anthony O'Hare)

Use a 2 × 1 rectangle of paper, with the same colour both sides. Make the centre creases. Fold the shorter edges to centre, crease and return.

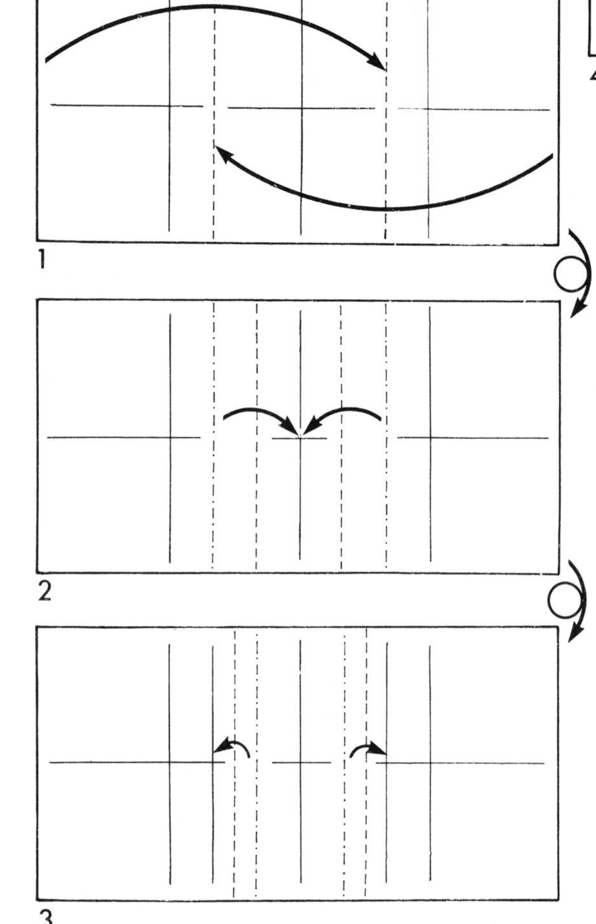

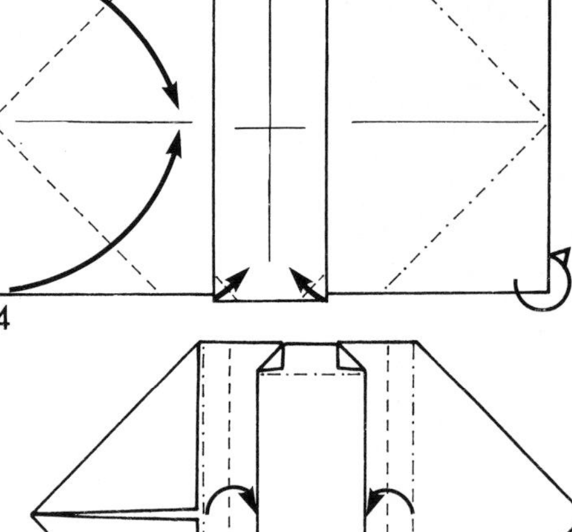

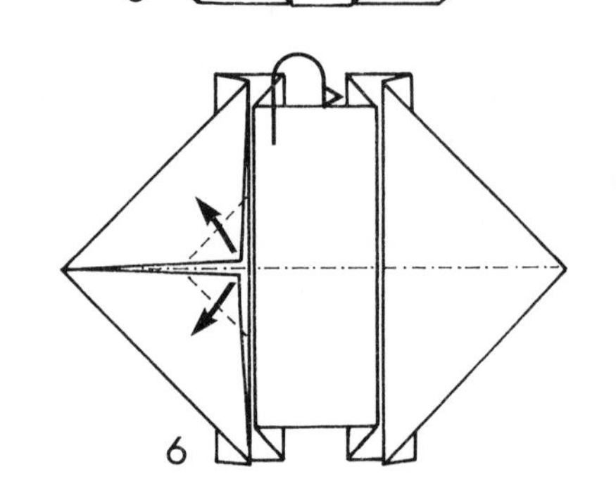

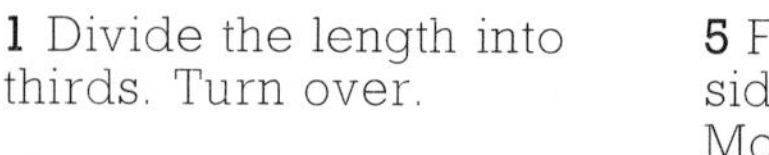

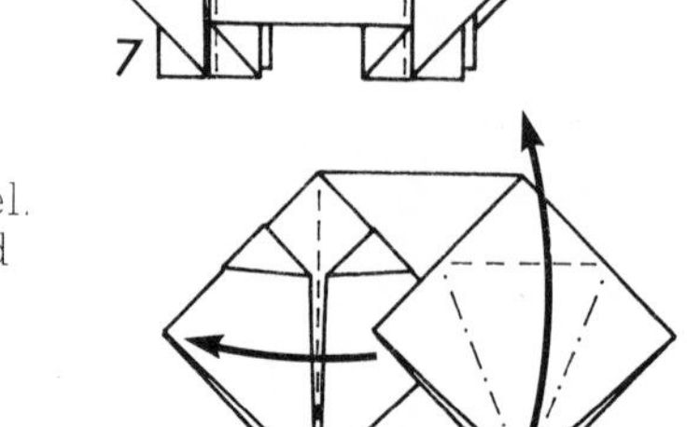

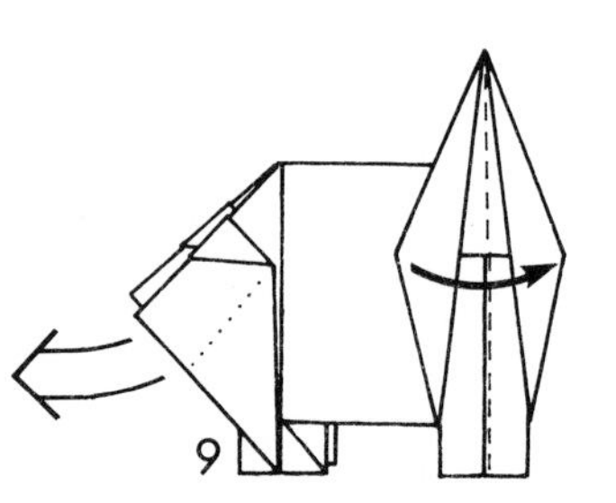

1 Divide the length into thirds. Turn over.

2 Pleat the one-third lines to the centre line and return. Turn over.

3 Pleat each crease made in step 2 to its nearest one-third line.

4 Fold the left corners to the horizontal centre line. Mountain fold the right corners to the centre line behind. Fold the four little corners of the centre panel.

5 Form pleats at the sides of the centre panel. Mountain fold at top and bottom.

6 Fold the triangular flaps. Mountain fold the paper in half.

7 Squash fold at left and right.

8 Valley fold at left. Petal fold at right.

9 Inside reverse fold the concealed flap at left. Fold right flap in half.

10 Mountain fold at left; repeat behind. Inside reverse fold the point at top right.

11 Inside reverse fold at left to form snout. Pull up point to form ear. Repeat behind. Inside reverse fold at right, and repeat behind, to narrow tail.

12 Put crimps in the tail.

13 Front trotters: swivel at left and mountain fold at right. Repeat behind.

14 Rear trotters: mountain fold. Repeat behind.

15 The pig completed.

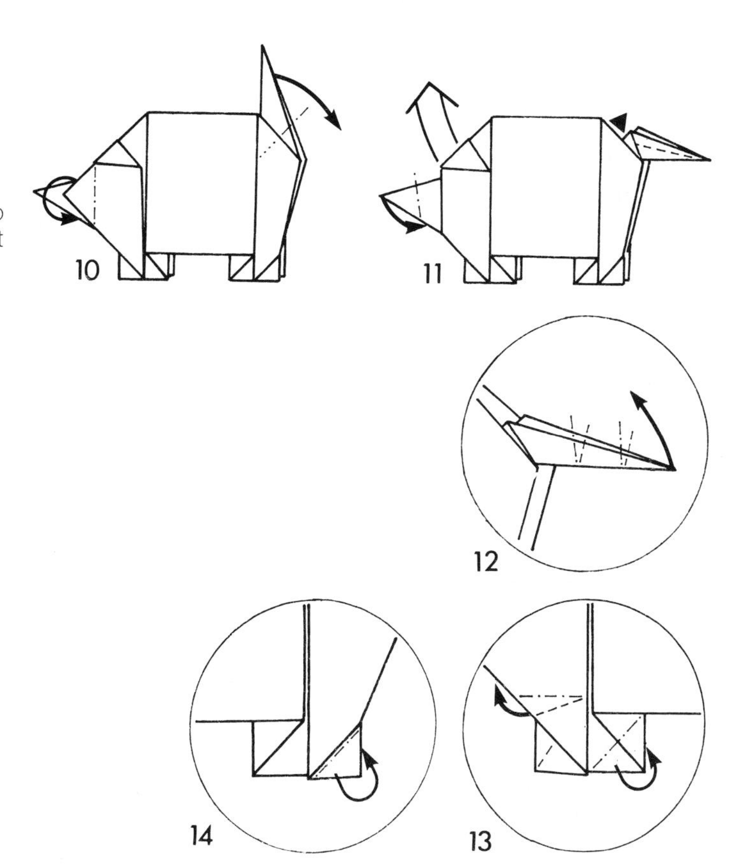

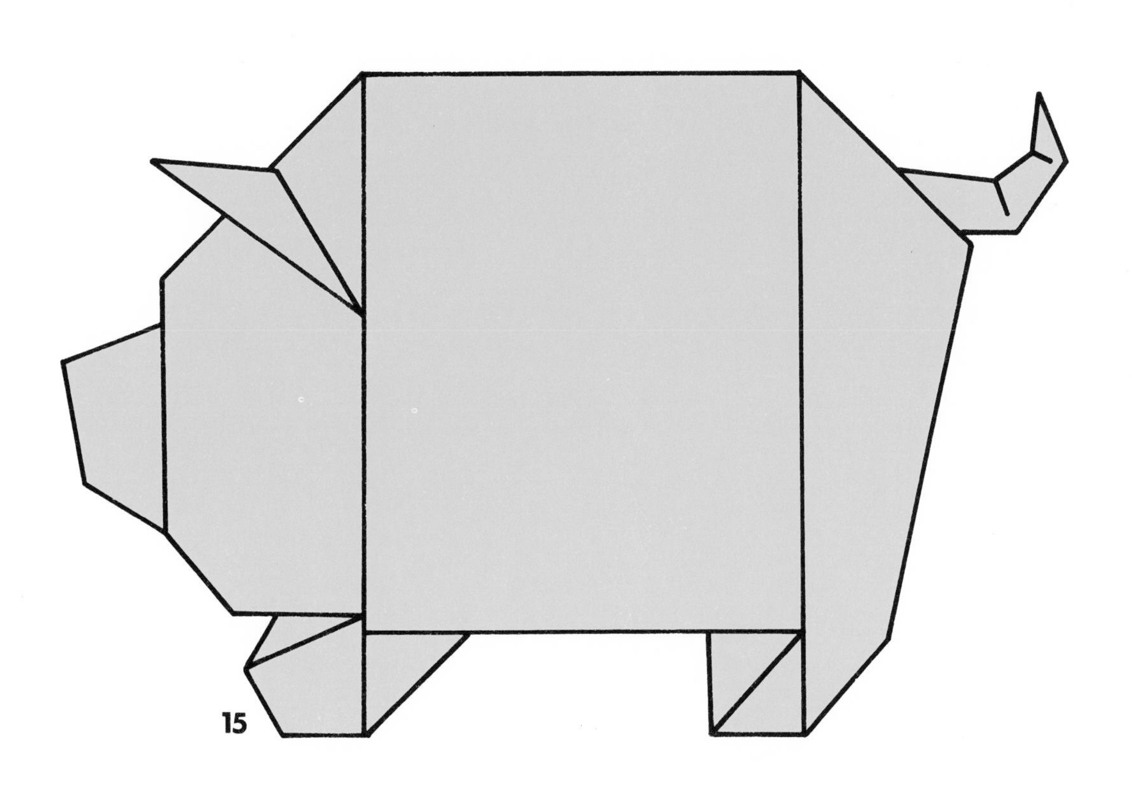

PIG TROUGH (Martin Wall)

Use a rectangle of paper about 2 × 3, white side up. Make the centre crease.

1 Fold the top and bottom edges to the centre.

2 Reverse fold the four corners.

3 Fold the four little flaps across.

4 Swing the side points behind, and the four front flaps forward, 90°. Rotate to new position.

5 Take the side point of one end flap to the top . . .

6 . . . like this. Crease firmly and return.

7 Now tuck the little flap into the pocket. Repeat at other end.

8 The pig trough completed.

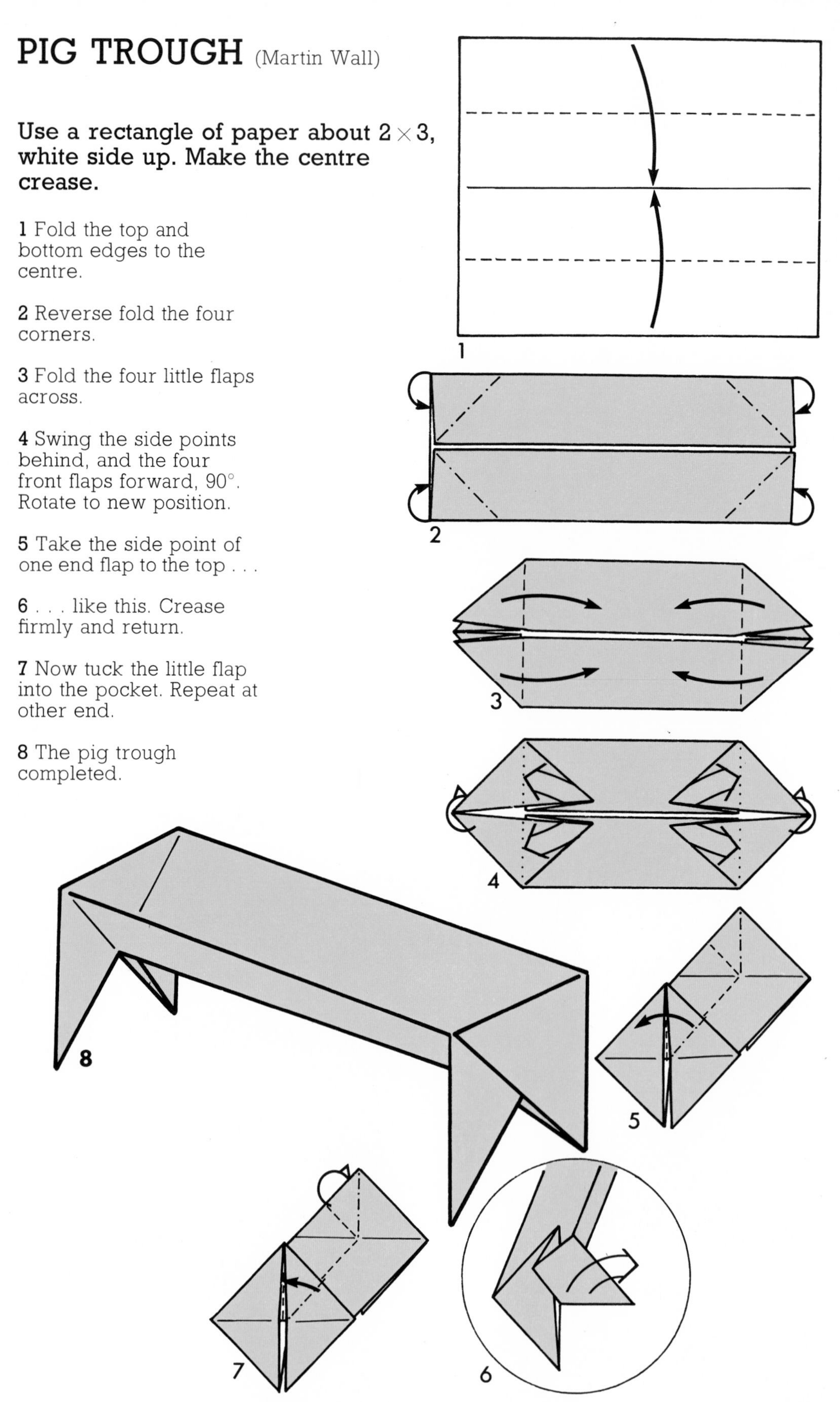

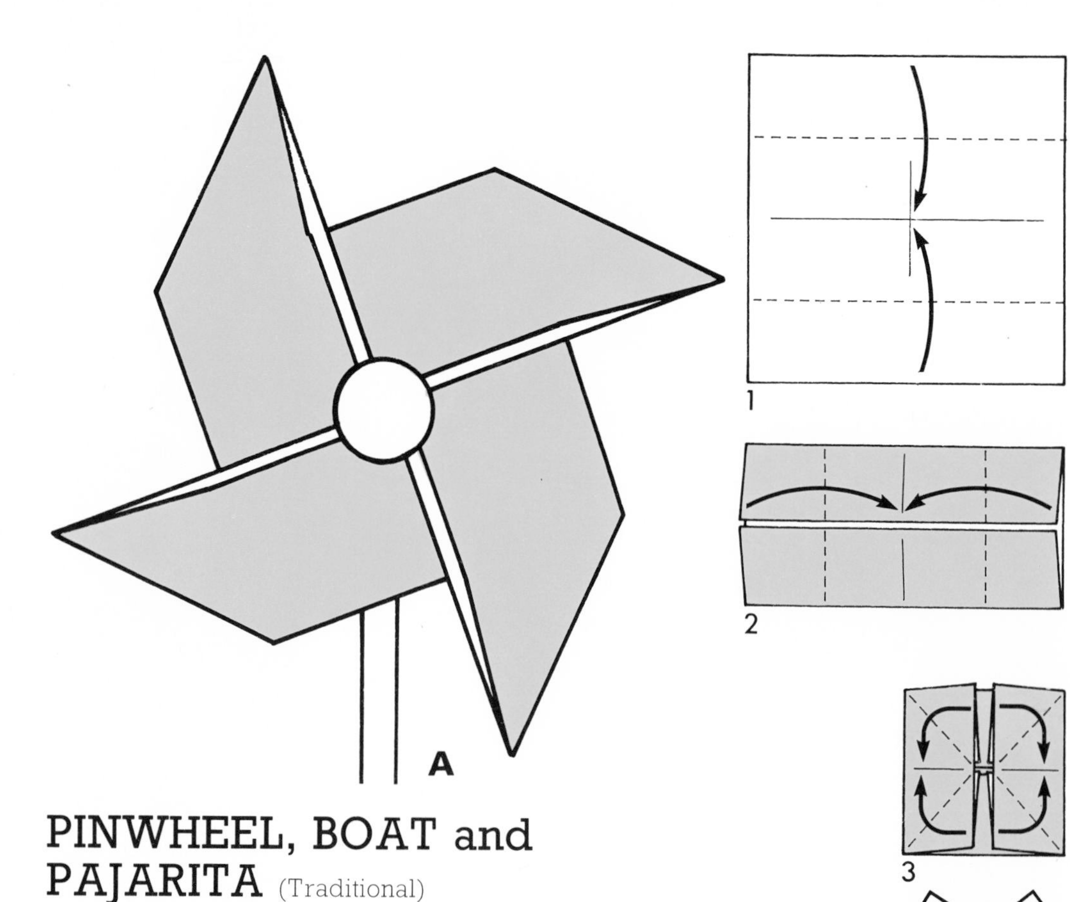

PINWHEEL, BOAT and PAJARITA (Traditional)

Use a square of paper, white side up. Mark the centre lines.

1 Fold the top and bottom edges to the centre.

2 Fold the sides to the centre.

3 Fold the four corners at top and bottom centre to centre left and right.

4 Lightly hold each flap between finger and thumb and pull the outer layer only up or down.

5 This is the result. Fold top right flap to right and bottom left flap to left.

6 When this form is pinned to a stick, it becomes a pinwheel which will spin when blown (fig. A). Mountain fold diagonally in half.

7 Rearrange three flaps . . .

8 . . . to form a simple boat with sail (fig. B). Outside reverse fold the left point.

9 When rotated, this form becomes the 'pajarita' (fig. C), or little Spanish bird, which is the earliest recorded folded paper toy to emerge in Europe.

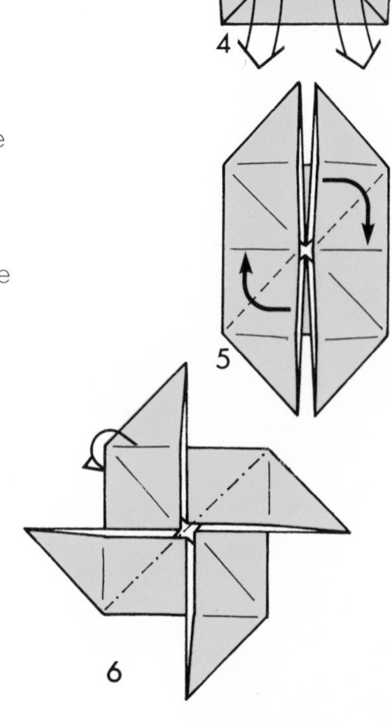

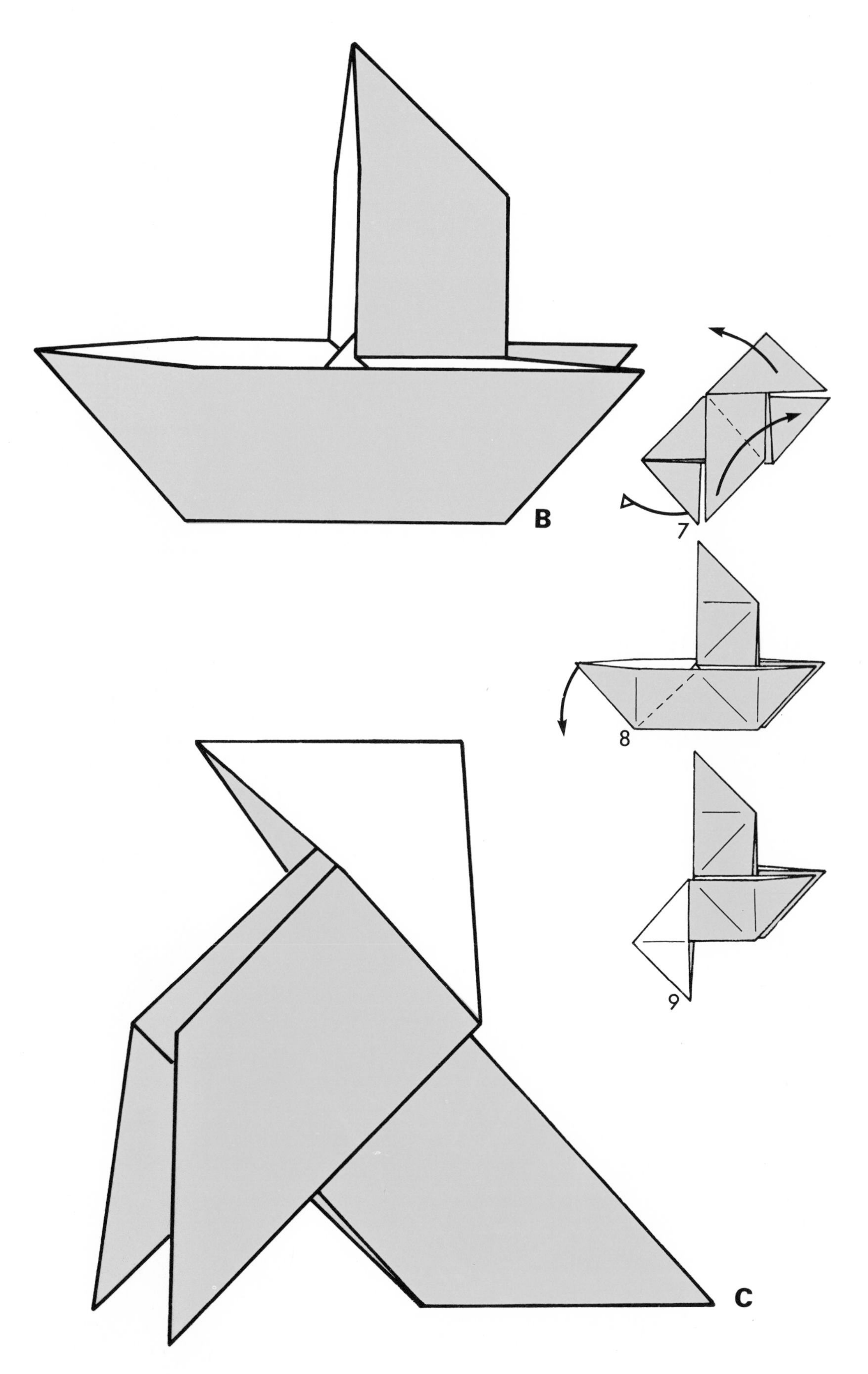
B
7
8
9
C

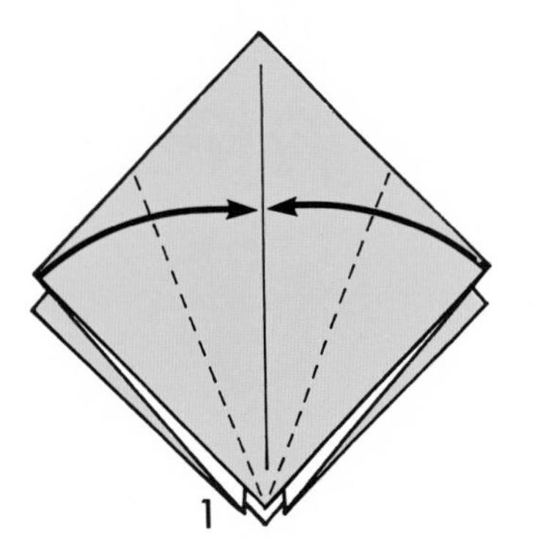

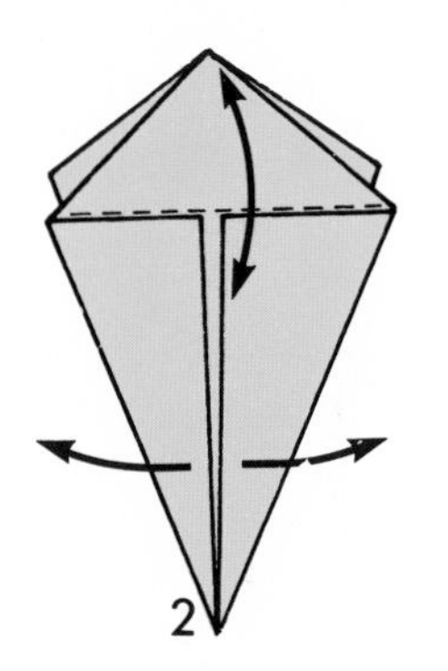

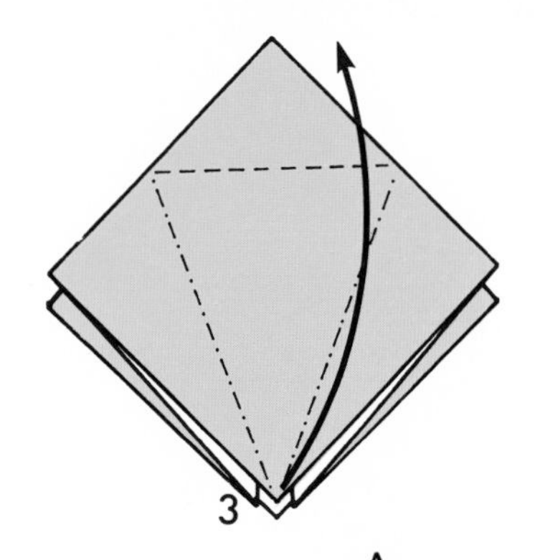

FLAPPING BIRD (Traditional)

Use a square of paper and complete steps 1–3 of the flower vase (page 22). Rotate so that the raw edges are at the bottom.

1 Fold the bottom left and right sides to the vertical centre crease. Repeat behind.

2 Fold the top triangular area down over the horizontal folded edges, crease firmly and return. Unfold to fig. 1.

3 Petal fold. Repeat behind.

4 Take the right flap across to the left. Repeat behind.

5 Fold the bottom point to the top. Repeat behind.

6 Pull the two inner flaps down in turn . . .

7 . . . to make this shape. Crease firmly at bottom. Inside reverse fold the left point.

8 This completes the bird. Curl the wings slightly between your thumb and forefinger. Hold the base of the neck and pull the tail: the bird's wings will flap.

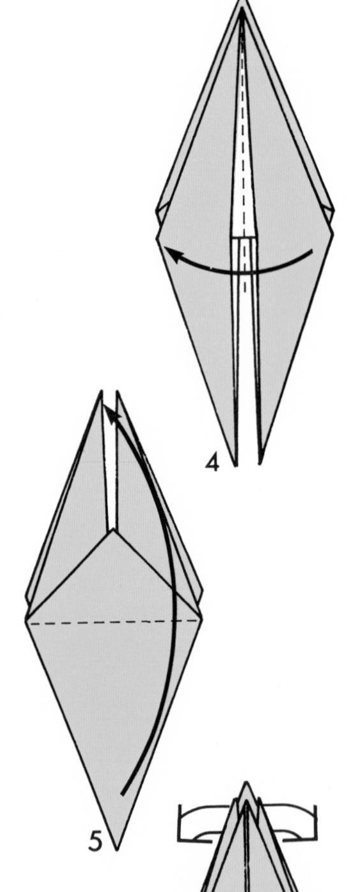

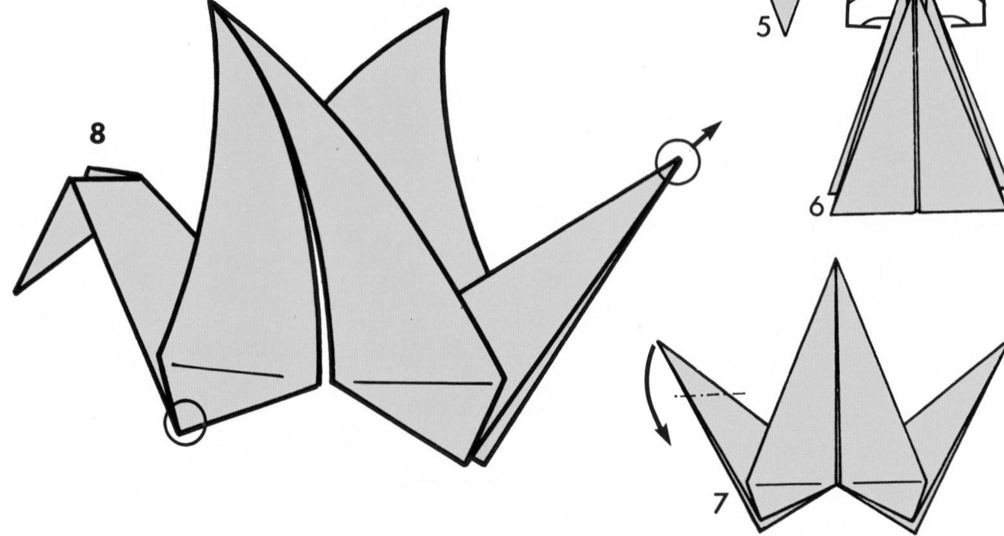

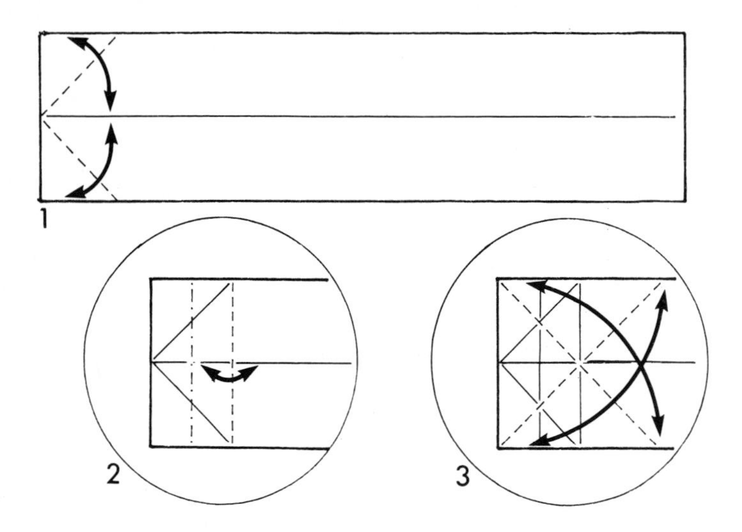

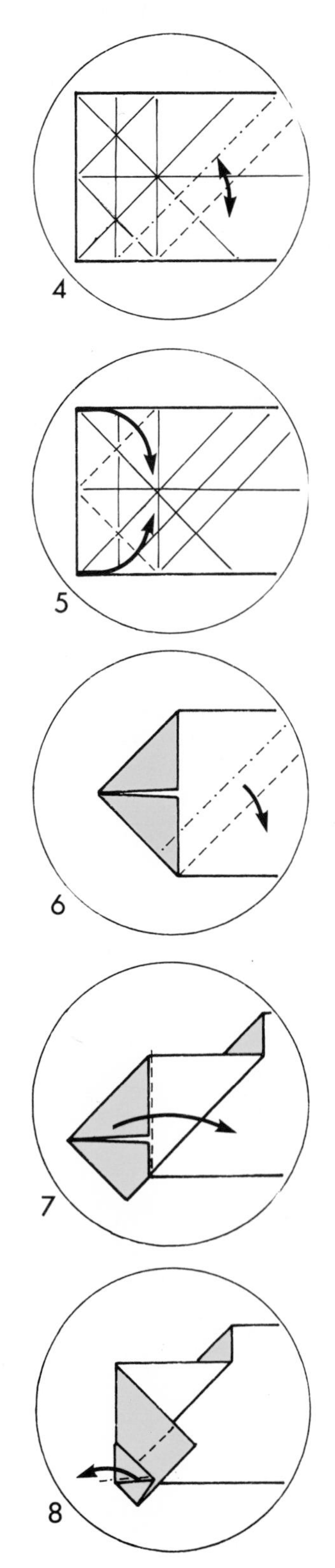

PAJARITA GREETING CARD (Jacques Justin)

Use a 4 × 1 rectangle of paper, white side up. Make the horizontal centre crease line.

1 Fold the left corners to centre line, crease and return.

2 Pleat (first fold on a vertical line between the ends of the existing creases, then fold raw edge to folded edge), crease and return.

3 Fold the left edge to top and bottom edges in turn. Crease and return.

4 Pleat, crease and return. This concludes the pre-creasing.

5 Fold left corners to centre line.

6 Pleat, using existing crease lines.

7 Fold coloured area to right.

8 Fold and unsquash point to left.

9 Fold point to angle.

10 Fold edge to angle.

11 Pull out concealed flap.

12 Mountain fold the top edge to bottom.

13 Fold on a vertical line about halfway between points A and B.

14 Fold in half from left to right.

15 Notice where the diagonal folded edge meets the vertical edge of the under flap; call this point C. Call the equivalent point on the upper flap point D and mountain fold the upper layer only of this flap.

16 Now slide the upper flap in behind the pajarita.

17 Mountain fold in half.

18 The completed card.

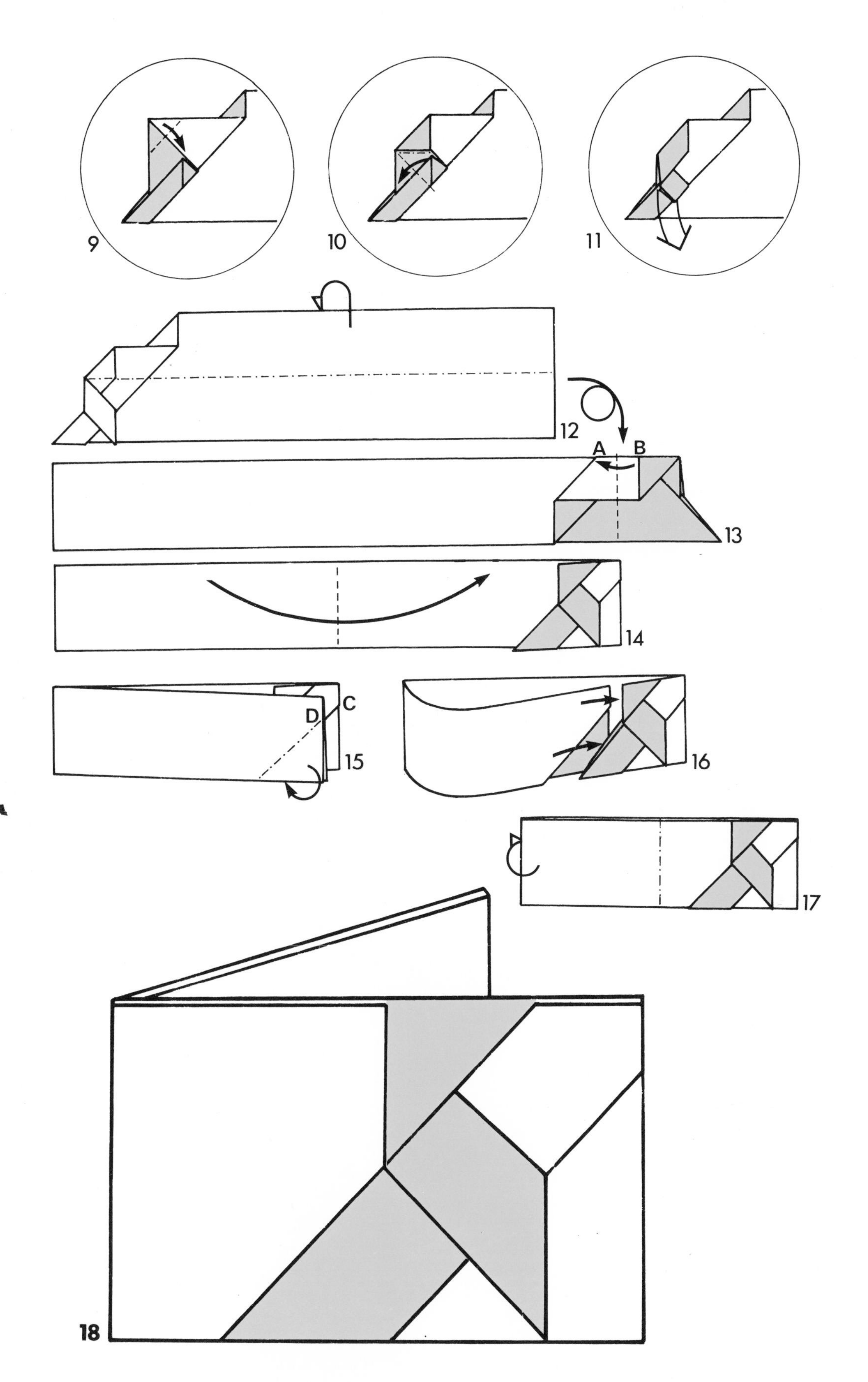
9
10
11
12
A
B
13
14
C
D
15
16
17
18

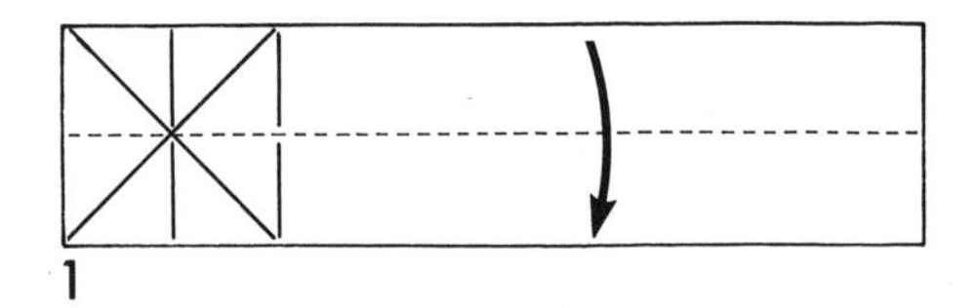

FLAPPING BIRD GREETING CARD (Jacques Justin)

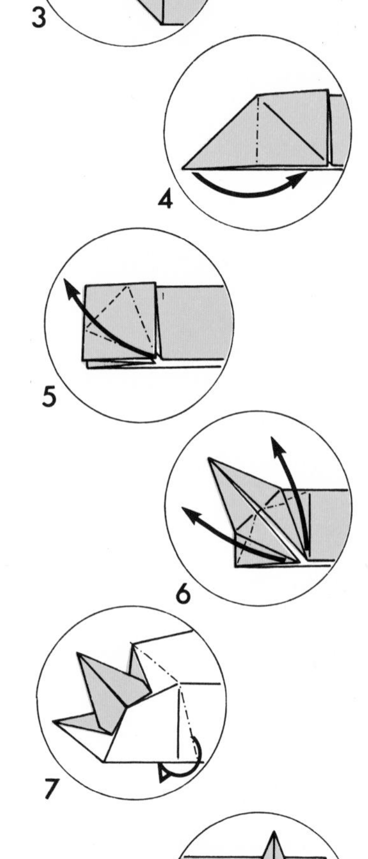

Use a rectangle of paper fractionally less than 1 × 4 (10 cm × 38.3 cm or 3.9 in × 15.1 in is ideal), white side up. First make the crease lines at left.

1 Fold top edge to bottom.

2 Fold up on existing crease line.

3 Lift upper layer and squash point to left.

4 Inside reverse fold.

5 Petal fold.

6 Two inside reverse folds.

7 The top edge of the paper has now moved into a different plane. Mountain fold to the left . . .

8 . . . and the paper is again in one plane. Inside reverse fold bottom edge to top.

9 Fold down wing.

10 Inside reverse fold head.

11 Mountain fold under layer of head.

12 Fold in half, taking left edge behind the bird.

13 Mountain fold in half.

14 The completed flapping bird card.

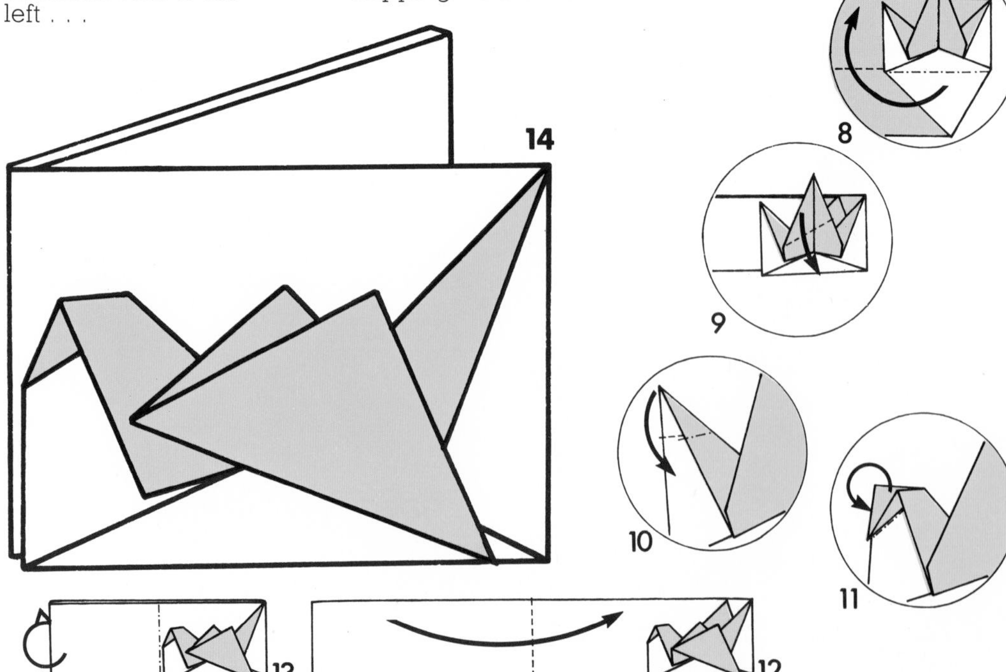

BOTTLE (Dave Brill)

To make a transparent bottle, use a square of thin acetate (Libra-Protecta film is good), but, as this does not fold very easily, use a square of paper for your first attempt. Divide into eighths horizontally.

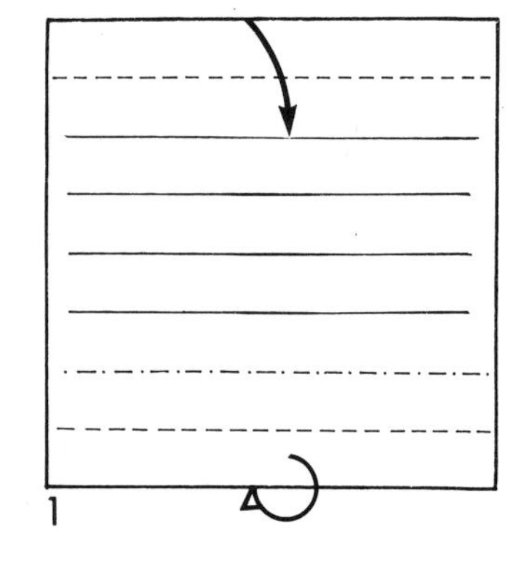

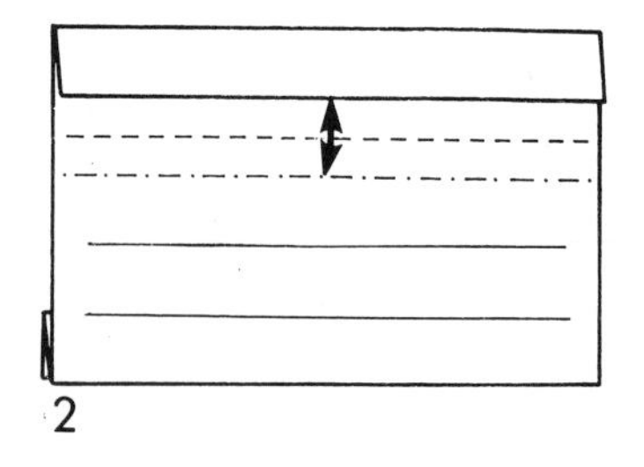

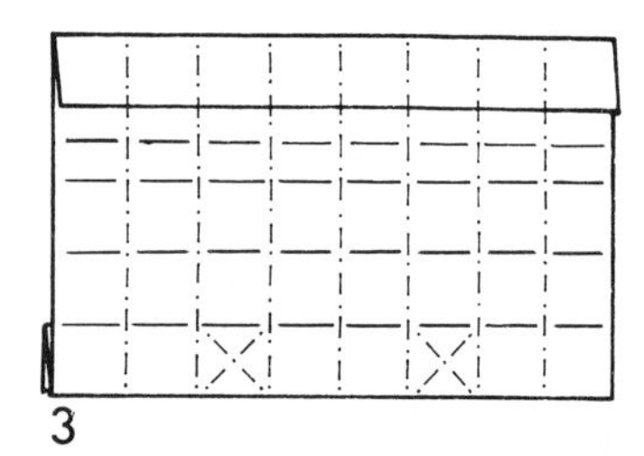

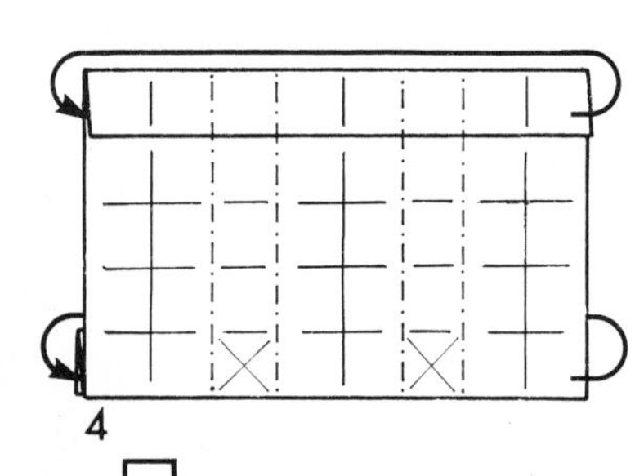

1 Fold down the top edge. Pleat behind at bottom.

2 Pleat the existing crease to the raw edge, crease firmly and return.

3 Divide into eighths vertically by mountain folding. Also mountain fold the diagonals of the two little squares, crease and return.

4 Form a rectangular tube by overlapping one side with the other. Interlock at top and bottom.

5 Push in the sides . . .

6 . . . to reach this shape. Rotate.

7 Form the neck by raising the front and back sides and then folding at left and right.

8 Bring the concealed raw edge to the front. Repeat behind.

9 Fold the top edge of each little inside flap down into its corner (this is to help the neck keep its shape). Turn upside down.

10 Fold down the inner layer at left into a horizontal plane.

11 Then fold down the inner layer at right.

12 Finally, fold the four edges down into the bottle. Turn right way up.

13 Use the box (page 14) as a cap for your bottle. The size of paper used to form the cap should be about three-eighths of that used to form the bottle.

A ship can be put into the bottle between steps 9 and 10.

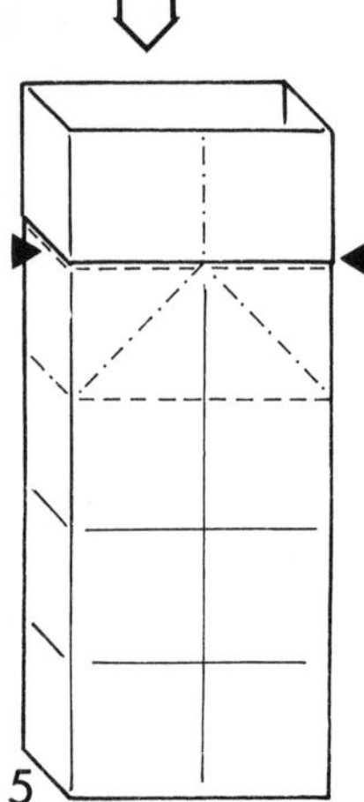

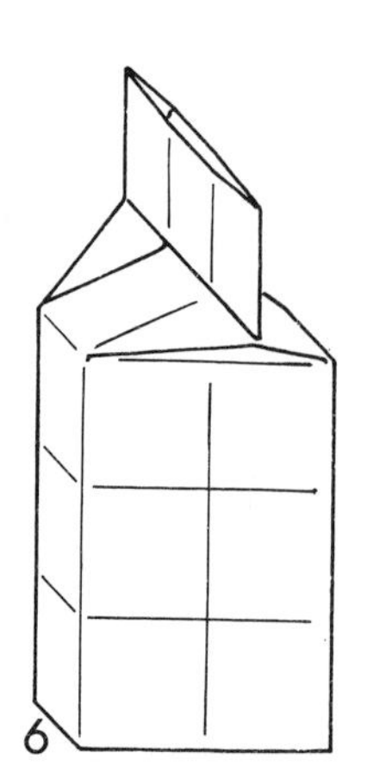

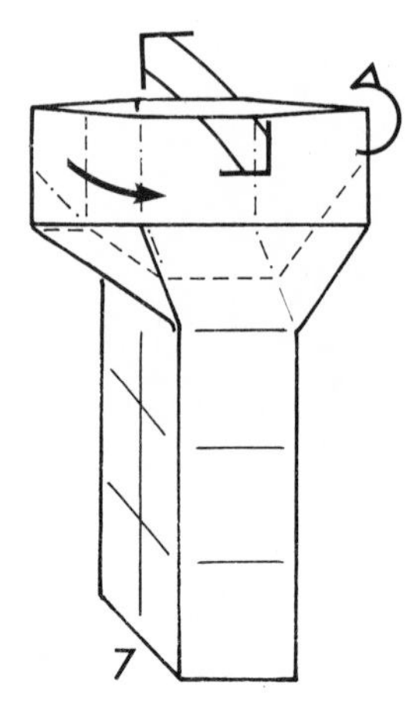

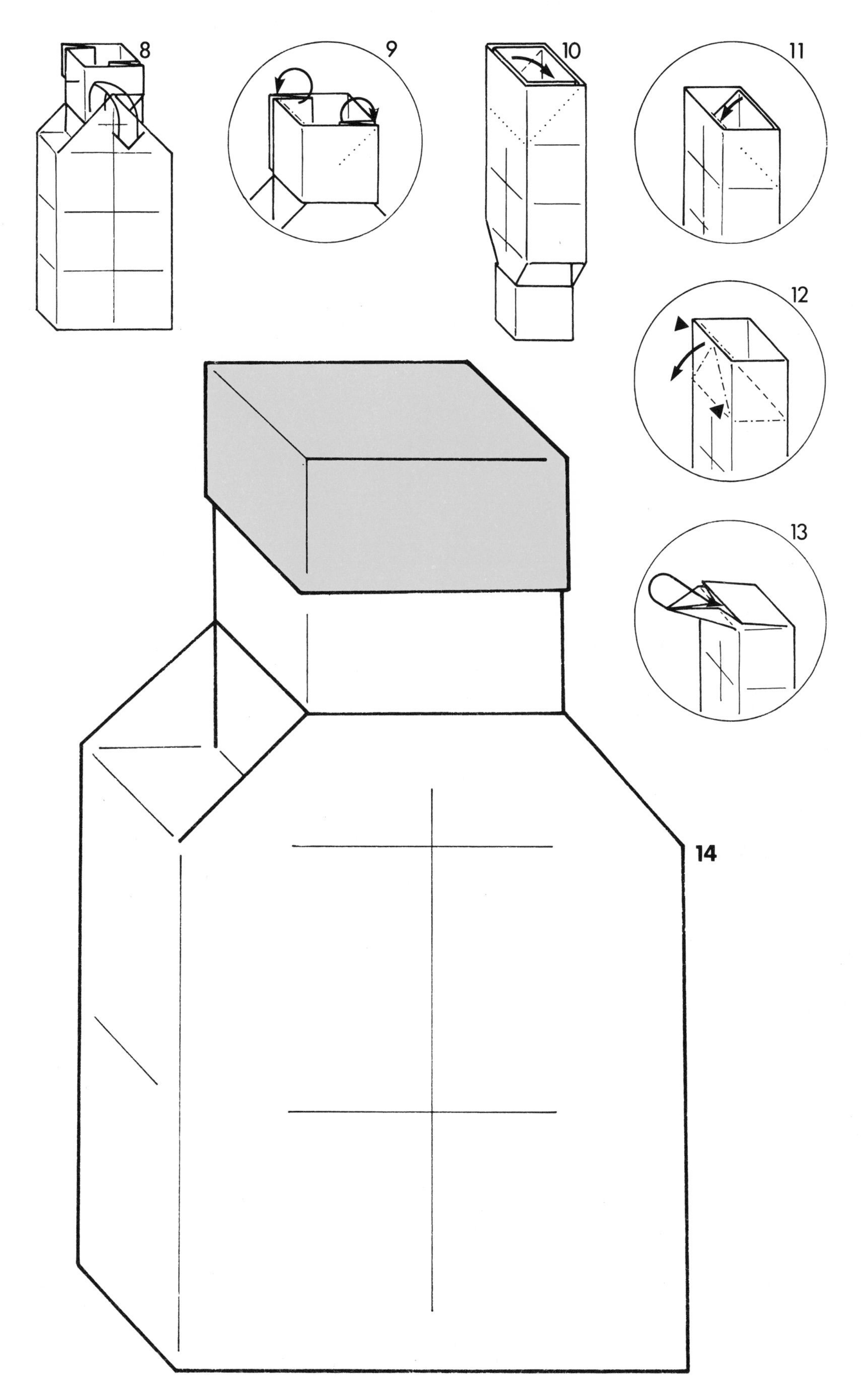
8
9
10
11
12
13
14

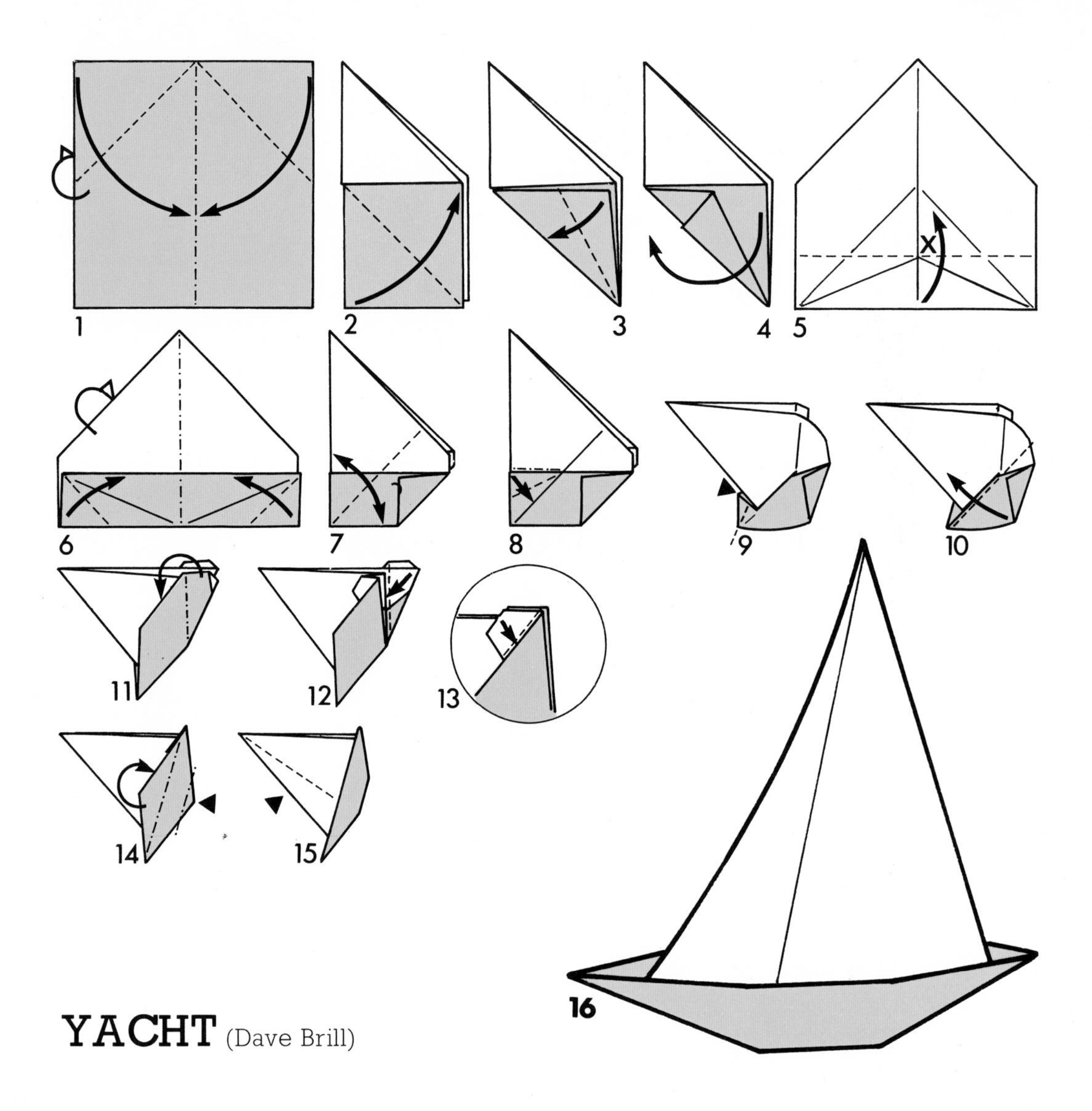

YACHT (Dave Brill)

Use a square of paper, coloured side up. Find the centre point.

1 Fold the top corners to the centre, then mountain fold in half.

2 Fold the bottom left corner to top right of the coloured area.

3 Fold the corner back to the folded edge. Crease firmly.

4 Partly unfold and open up . . .

5 . . . like this. Fold up the bottom edge on a horizontal line, through point X.

6 Fold bottom corners to the raw edge. Mountain fold in half.

7 Fold the bottom edge (top layer only) to the vertical folded edge, crease and return. Repeat behind.

8 Now bring the raw coloured edge down to the crease line made in step 7 . . .

9 . . . and put a fold in the small rear flap so that the new shape is held firm.

10 Fold up the bottom point. Repeat behind and flatten.

11 Reverse fold at right.

12 Tuck the rear flap into the reverse fold.

13 Tuck in surplus paper.

14 Mountain fold at left; repeat behind. Push in at right.

15 Run a finger down one edge to shape the sail.

16 The yacht completed.

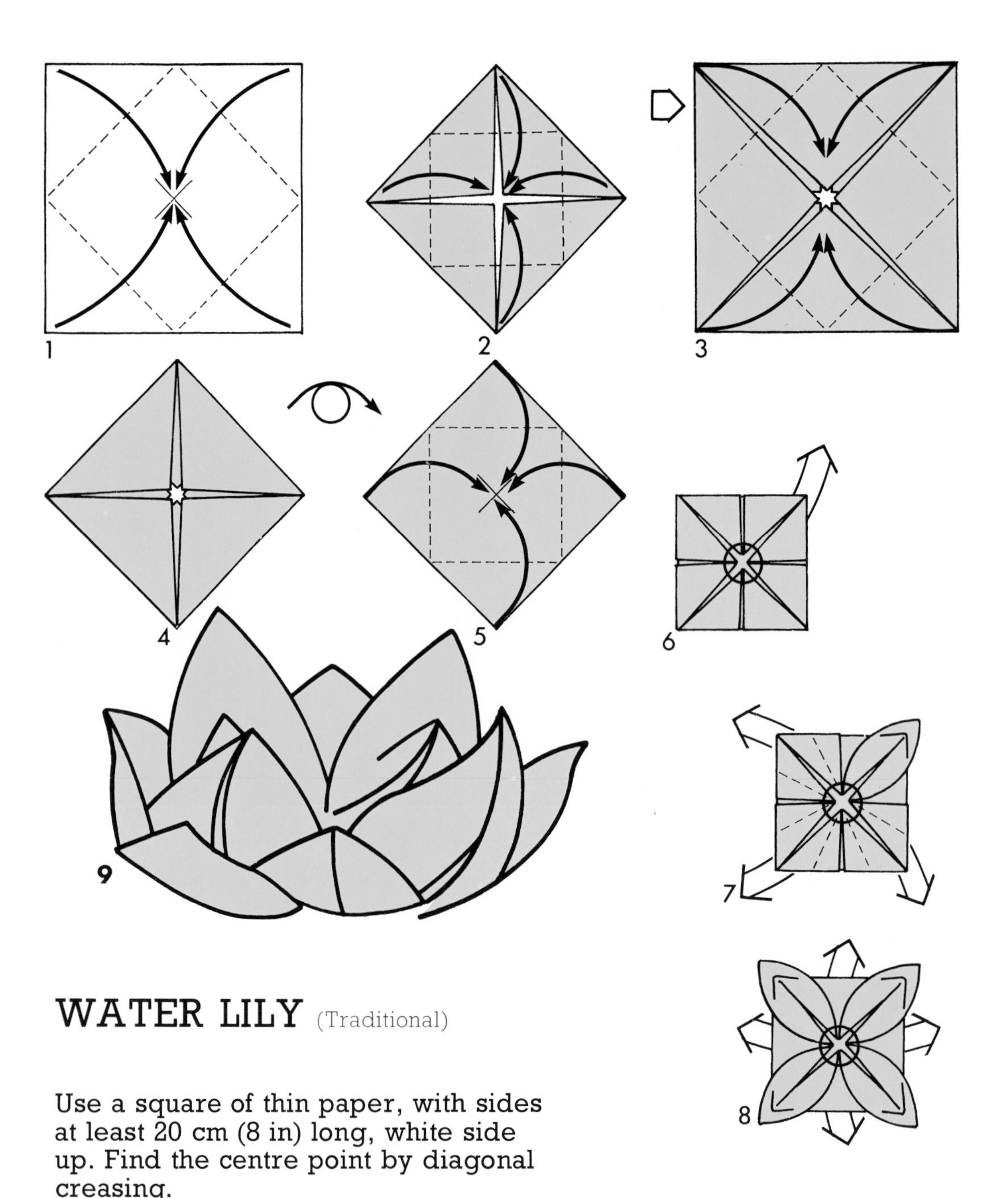

WATER LILY (Traditional)

Use a square of thin paper, with sides at least 20 cm (8 in) long, white side up. Find the centre point by diagonal creasing.

1 Fold each corner to the centre in turn.

2 Fold each new corner to the centre.

3 Again, fold each corner to the centre . . .

4 . . . and turn over.

5 Fold each corner to the centre.

6 Bring forward one point from behind. To do this you must raise the two adjacent front flaps as you raise the point, then return the flaps. Hold the centre front points in place with your thumb as you shape the point from behind into a petal . . .

7 . . . like this. Repeat on other three corners.

8 Continue to pull more points from behind to form petals. At first, keep your thumb on the centre points so that the flower will hold its shape.

9 The water lily completed. Paper or starched napkins can be folded in this way to serve as table decorations.

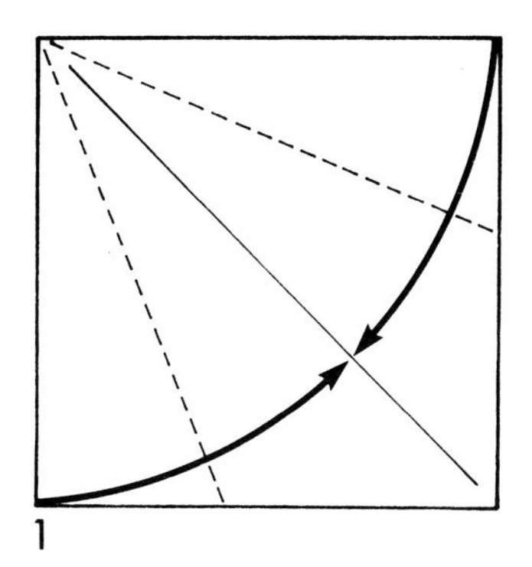

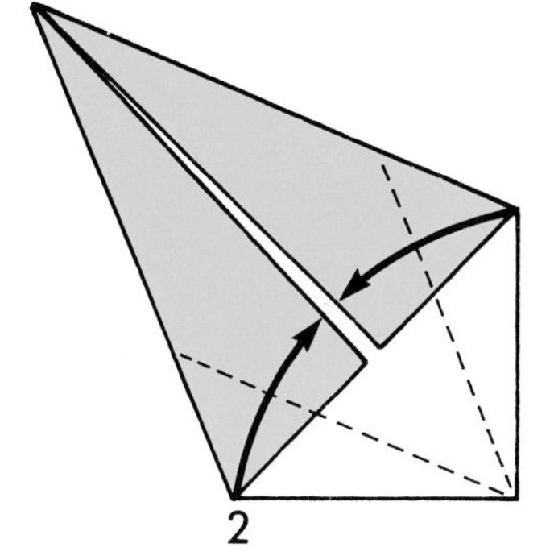

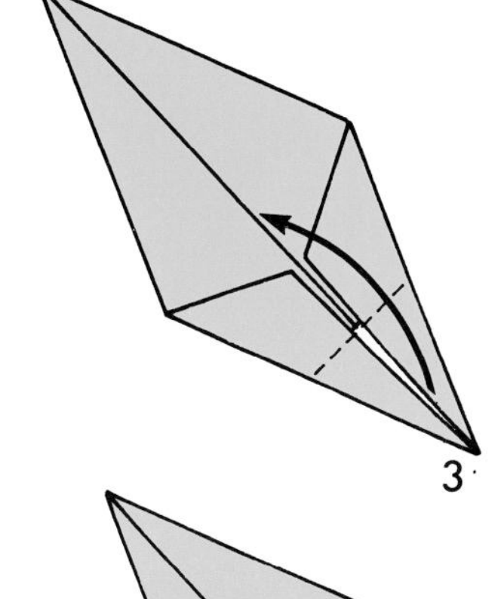

ROSE (Toshie Takahama)
Leaves

Use three squares of green paper, two with sides 10 cm (4 in) long and one with sides 12 cm (4.75 in) long. Fold each, in turn, in the following way. Start with the white side up and the diagonal crease line marked.

1 Fold left and top edges to the diagonal crease.

2 Fold bottom and right edges to the diagonal crease.

3 Fold the bottom right point over the concealed raw edge.

4 Fold the point back.

5 Form the leaf stem by folding the edges of the narrow section to the diagonal, squashing at top.

6 Fold in half.

7 Pleat . . .

8 . . . like this. Crease firmly and unpleat.

9 Glue the stem to a thin wire.

10 Join the three leaves together by binding the wires with green adhesive tape.

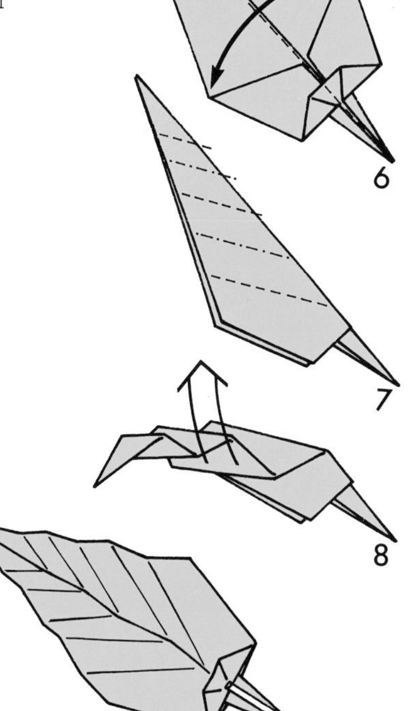

ROSE
Calyx

Use a 9 cm (3.5 in) square of green paper. Complete steps 1–3 of the flapping bird on page 40 and then continue as follows:

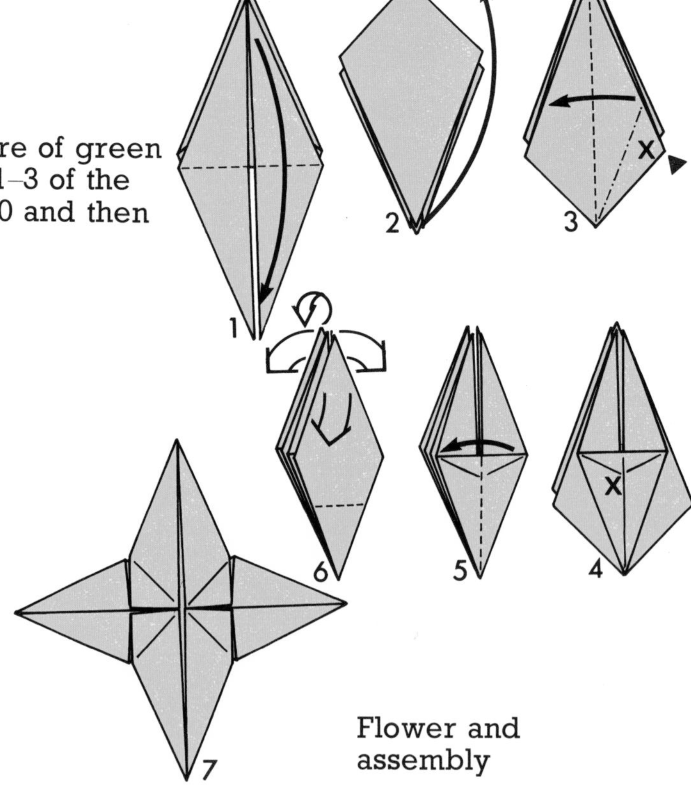

1 Fold the top point to the bottom. Repeat behind.

2 Rotate so that the four free points are at the top.

3 Raise the right flap and take the upper layer to the left, flattening point X . . .

4 . . . like this. Repeat on other three sides.

5 Take the right flap across to the left. Repeat behind.

6 Pull the top points out as far as they will go . . .

7 . . . like this. This completes the calyx.

Flower and assembly

1 Use five squares of coloured tissue paper with sides 30 cm, 25 cm, 20 cm, 15 cm and 10 cm (or 12 in, 10 in, 8 in, 6 in and 4 in) long. Make five separate water lilies (page 50), one from each square, and then put them inside each other to make the flower. Curl the petals outwards slightly.

For the stem, use a knitting needle or thick wire; twist a scrap of paper, of the kind used for the flowers, around the top end and fix it there with a drop of glue. Assemble the rose by pushing the needle or wire through the flower from the top and pushing the calyx up from the bottom.

2 Fix the leaves to the stem by winding green adhesive tape around its length. This completes the rose.

1

2

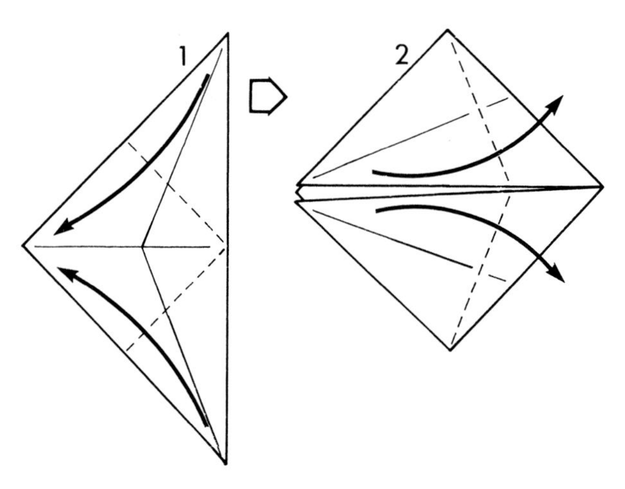

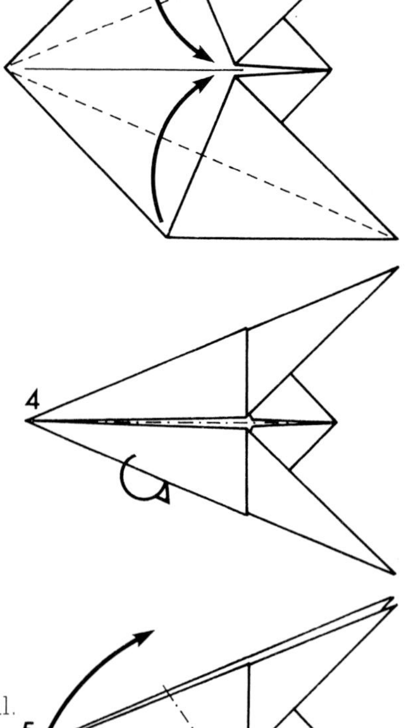

SWAN (John French)

Use a right-angled triangle (a square cut diagonally in half) of white paper. Fold all the edges together in turn to make the crease lines.

1 Fold the right corners to the left.

2 Fold the two flaps to the right so that their outer edges lie parallel to centre crease.

3 Fold on existing crease lines.

4 Mountain fold in half.

5 Inside reverse fold left point up.

6 Narrow the neck by folding in half. Repeat behind.

7 Fold top of wing to base line, releasing paper at left. Repeat behind.

8 Fold along folded edge. Repeat behind.

9 Inside reverse fold tail.

10 Squash fold wing. Repeat behind.

11 Outside reverse fold top point. Then mountain fold edge of wing into model. Repeat behind.

12 Outside reverse fold to form head.

13 Pull out concealed edge. Repeat behind.

14 Double reverse fold to form beak.

15 Inside reverse fold tip of beak.

16 The swan completed.

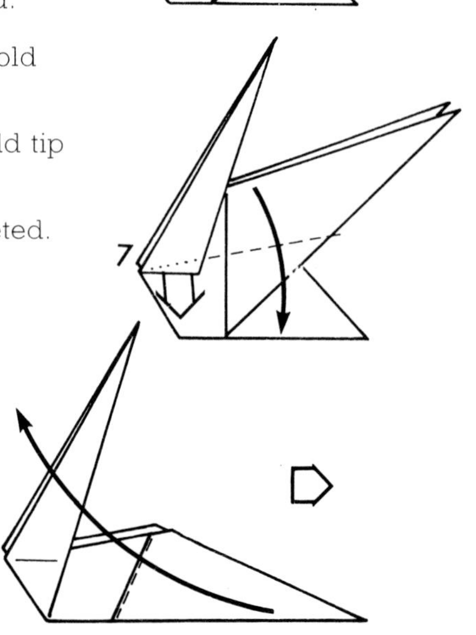

9
10
11
12
13
14
15
16

DUCK (David Venables)

Use a square of paper, white side up. Mark the centre crease.

1 Fold the two bottom edges to centre crease.

2 Fold the top edges to centre crease.

3 Mountain fold in half.

4 Inside reverse fold bottom point up.

5 Inside reverse fold right point down.

6 Inside reverse fold up.

7 Outside reverse fold left point.

8 Double reverse fold left point. Mountain fold bottom point into model and repeat behind.

9 The duck completed.

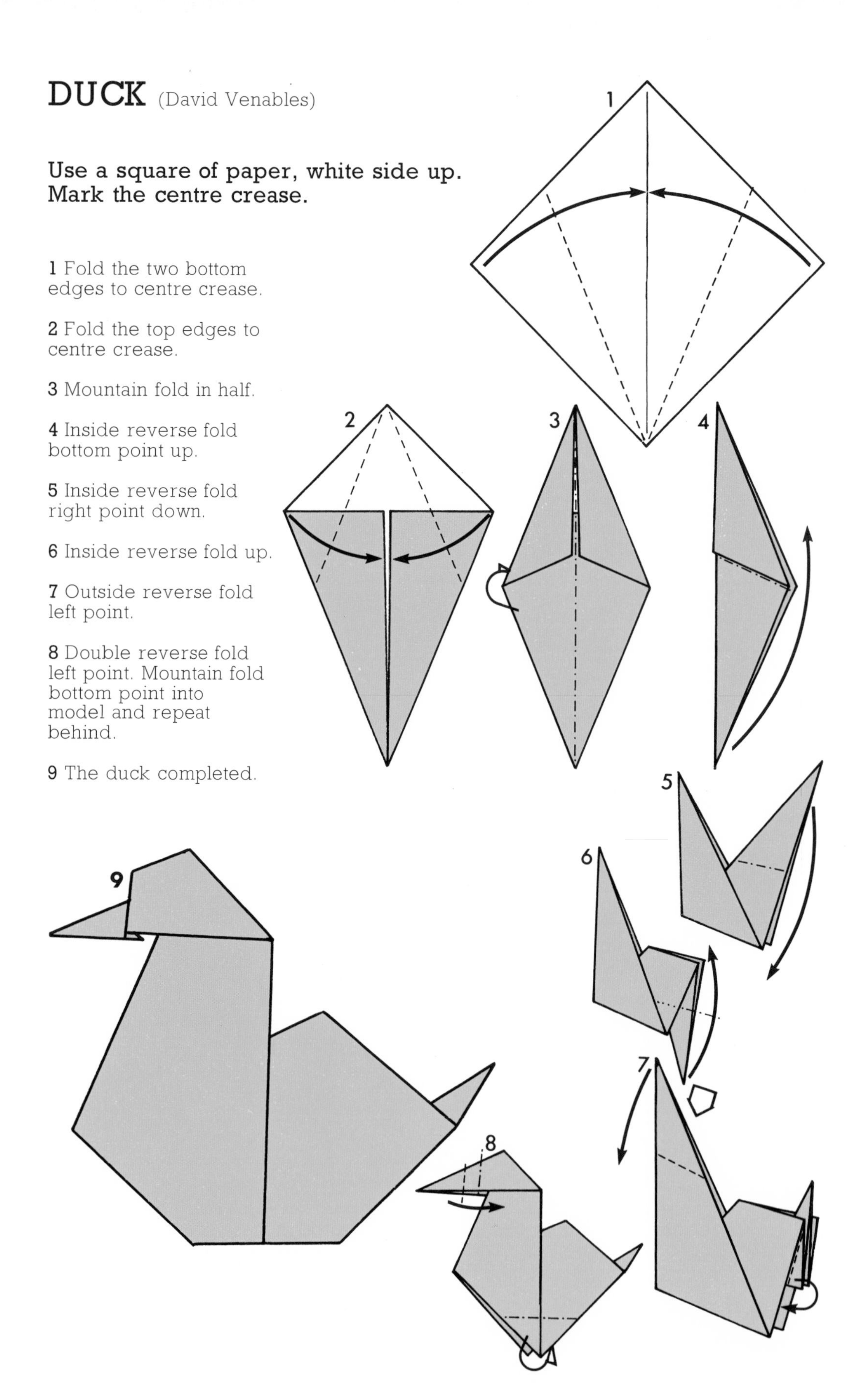

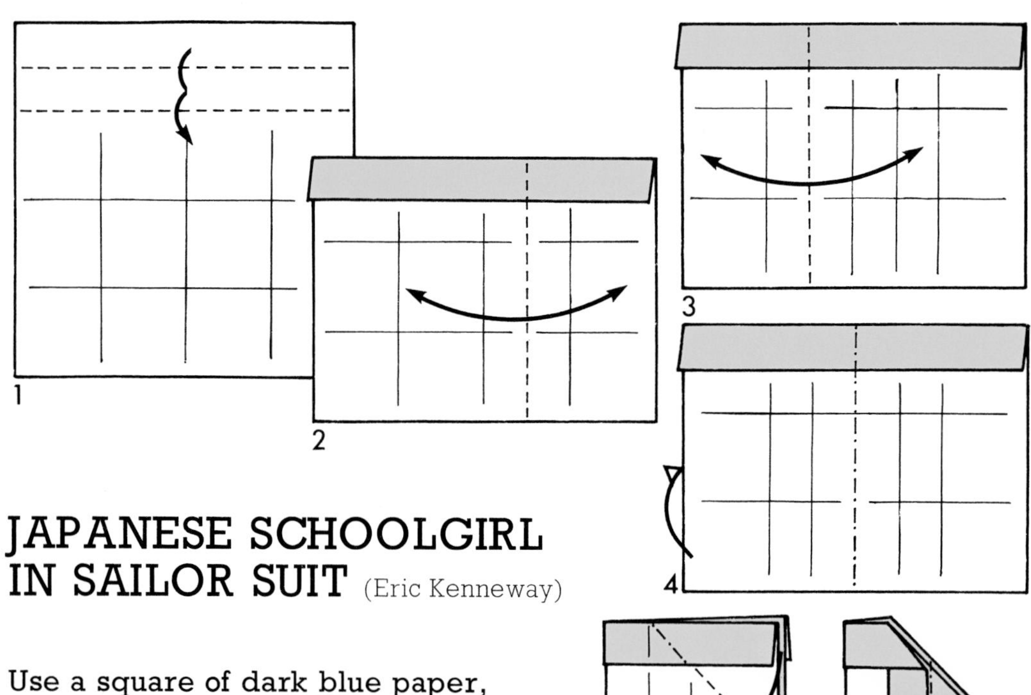

JAPANESE SCHOOLGIRL IN SAILOR SUIT (Eric Kenneway)

Use a square of dark blue paper, white side up. Mark the centre lines; then mark the quarter lines by folding each side to the centre in turn.

1 Fold the top edge to the quarter line and then fold over again.

2 Fold the right edge to the left quarter line and return.

3 Fold the left edge to the right quarter line and return.

4 Mountain fold in half.

5 Inside reverse fold the top right corner down to existing crease line. Repeat behind.

6 Inside reverse fold right edge to left. Repeat behind.

7 Swivel the collar to new position. Repeat behind.

8 Mountain fold projecting paper at right into model. Repeat behind.

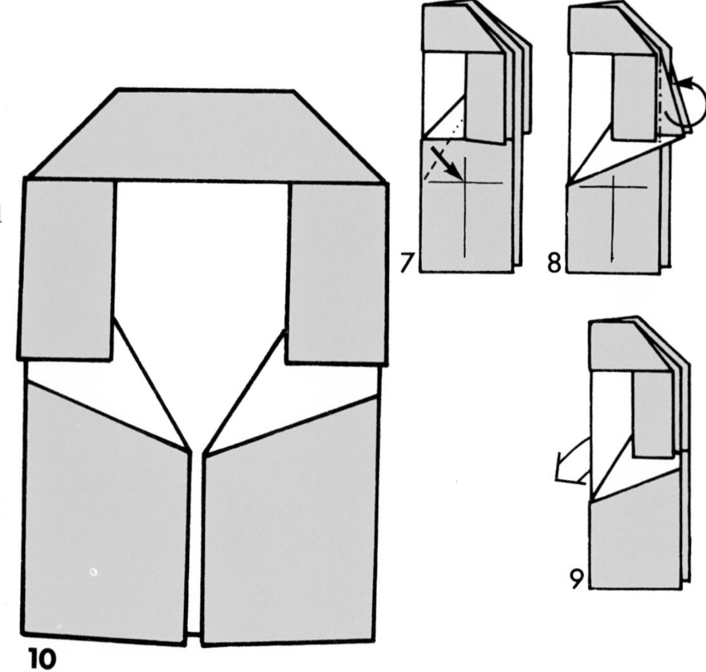

9 Bring rear flap from behind.

10 The completed Japanese schoolgirl in her sailor suit.

TWO MORE JAPANESE SCHOOLGIRLS

It can be fun to make a group of girls and to vary them by giving them different hairstyles. Here are two examples:

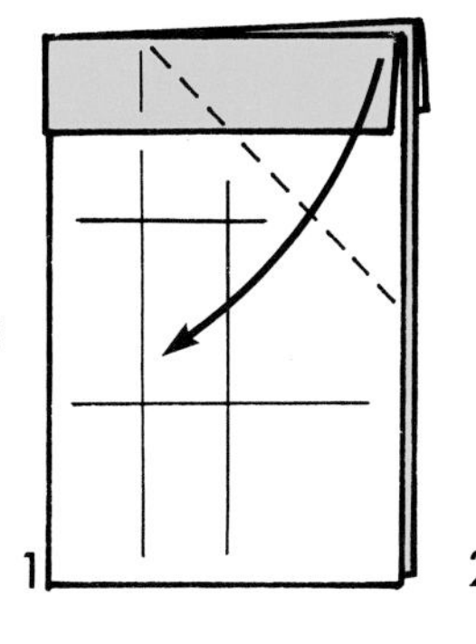

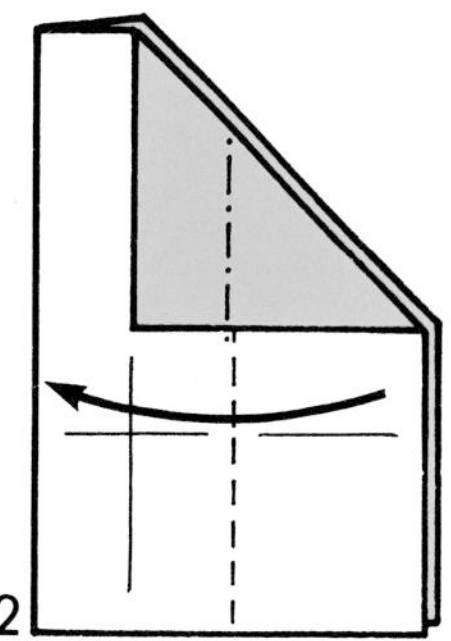

A
Complete steps 1–4 of the Japanese schoolgirl on page 58 and then continue as follows:

1 Valley fold the top right point to the existing crease line. Repeat behind.

2 Inside reverse fold right edge to left. Repeat behind.

3 Swivel collar to new position. Repeat behind.

4 Swivel the bottom of the hair to the edge of the collar. Repeat behind.

5 Pull out concealed point. Repeat behind.

6 Bring rear flap around to front.

7 Another Japanese schoolgirl completed.

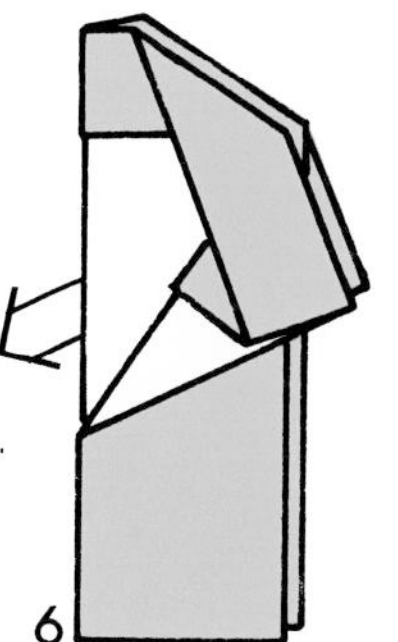

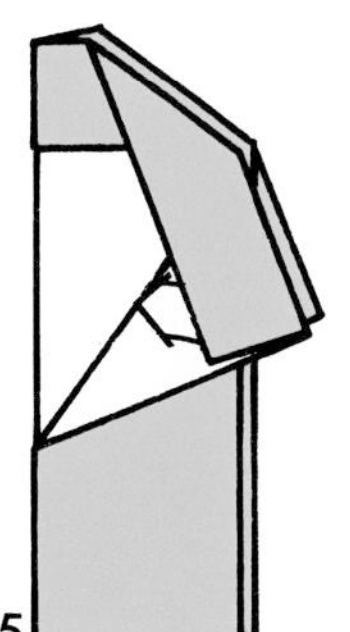

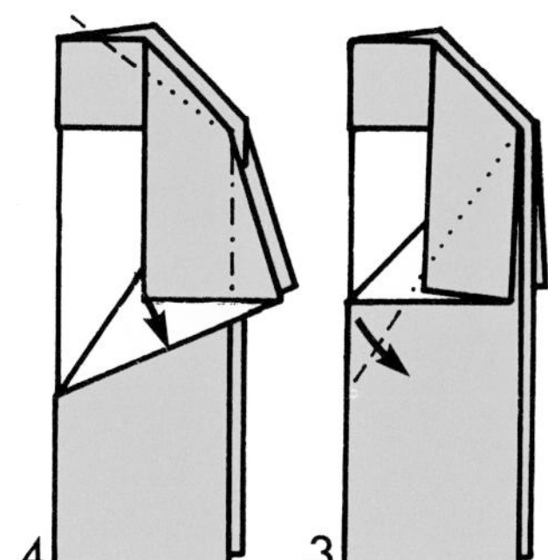

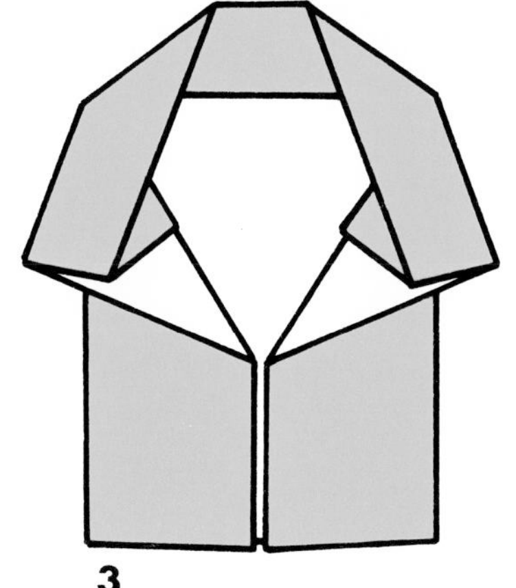

B
Complete steps 1–3 of the Japanese schoolgirl above, and then continue as follows:

1 Bring rear flap around to front.

2 Swivel the hair under at left.

3 A third Japanese schoolgirl completed.

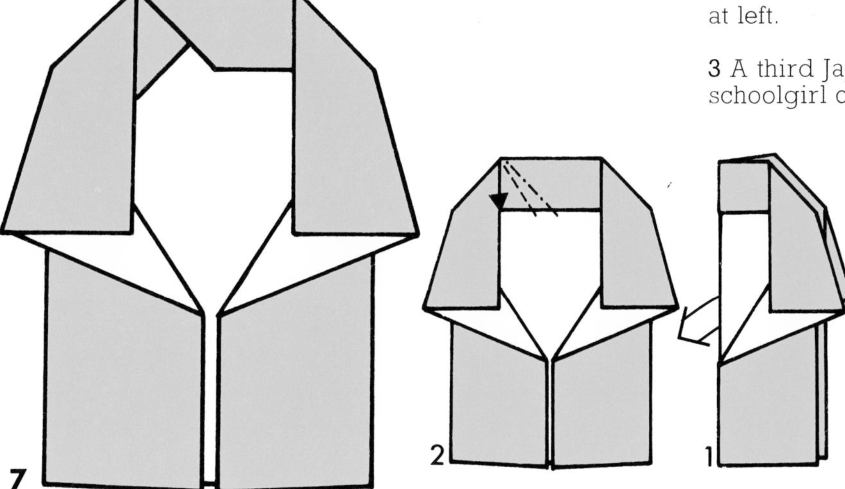

TREES ON A HILLSIDE (Eric Kenneway)

Use a square of green paper, coloured side up. First mark the diagonal creases.

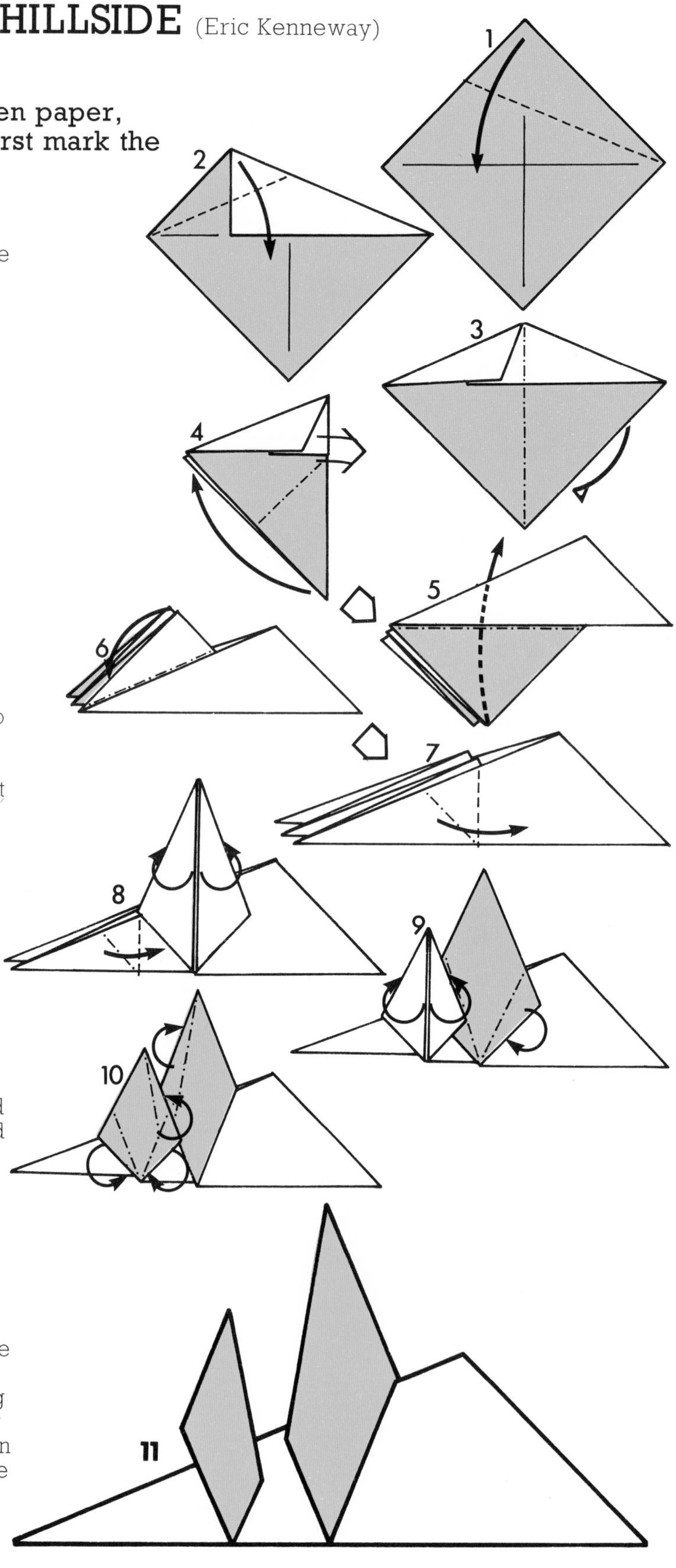

1 Fold the top right edge to the horizontal centre line.

2 Fold the top left edge to the horizontal centre line.

3 Mountain fold in half.

4 Pull out the concealed point at top. Inside reverse fold bottom point.

5 Inside reverse fold bottom point. Repeat behind.

6 Inside reverse fold top point. Repeat behind.

7 Squash fold uppermost layer at centre front.

8 Turn new flap inside out. To do this, open up the paper and alter the mountain fold edges of the flap into valley folds; then reform the model. Squash fold flap at left.

9 Turn this new flap inside out. Mountain fold lower edges of coloured flap to start forming tree.

10 Continue mountain folding edges of the coloured flaps to form trees.

11 The trees on a hillside completed. If you make several of these, varying the position and number of the trees, you can then fit them together to make a landscape frieze as a background for other models.

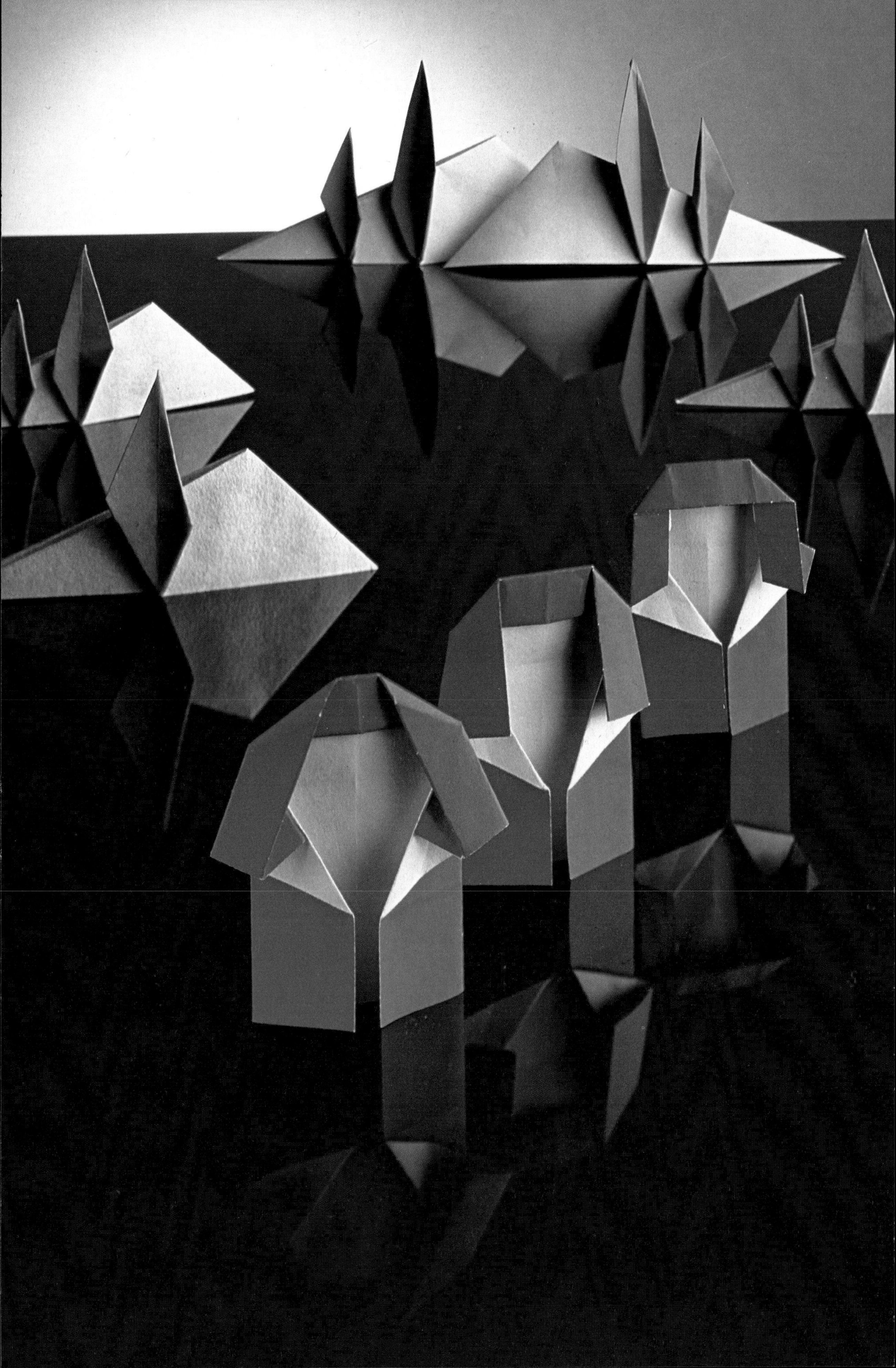

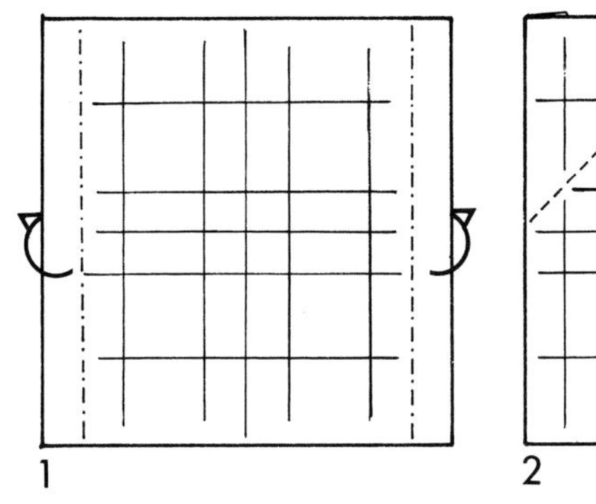

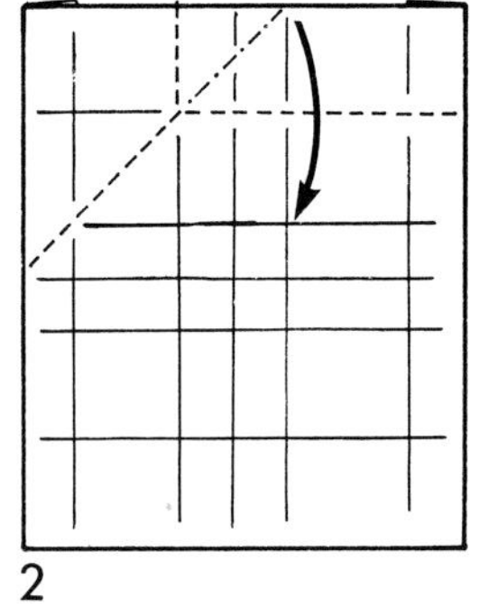

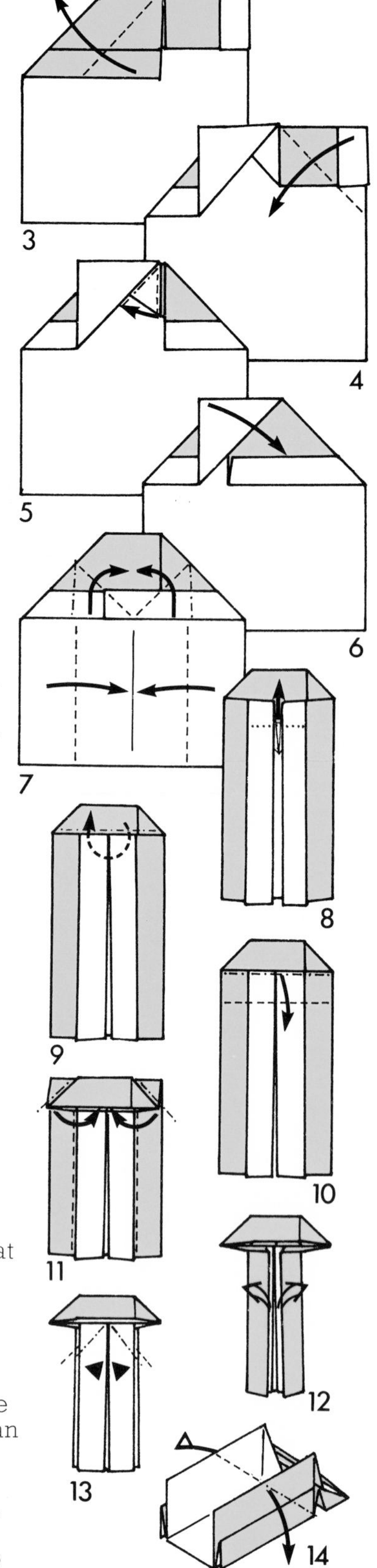

BOX WITH LID (Dave Brill)

Use a large square of paper, white side up. Divide the square into fifths, both widthways and lengthways, and mark the centre crease lines.

1 Mountain fold the left and right edges to the existing crease line behind.

2 Fold top left point and top edge down, creating an inside reverse fold at top centre.

3 Fold this flap up.

4 Fold top right corner down.

5 Swivel the inside flap up so that the vertical fold line meets the inside top edge.

6 Return the top flap and tuck it under the folded edge.

7 Fold the left and right sides to the centre, swivelling at top.

8 Fold the concealed point at the horizontal folded edge (to do this you will need to open the model slightly).

9 Mountain fold the concealed flap to the inside top edge (again, open the model slightly and raise the sides so that you can insert your fingers).

10 Pleat.

11 Fold the sides to the centre.

12 Pull out concealed raw edges to left and right.

13 Push against the vertical, folded centre edges to raise the sides . . .

14 . . . like this. Now flatten . . .

15 . . . like this. Swivel at left and right.

16 Turn the coloured side panels inside out.

17 Fold the bottom edge up to the top, creating an inside reverse fold.

18 Fold front flap down.

19 Swivel the left flap to the right and down into the model.

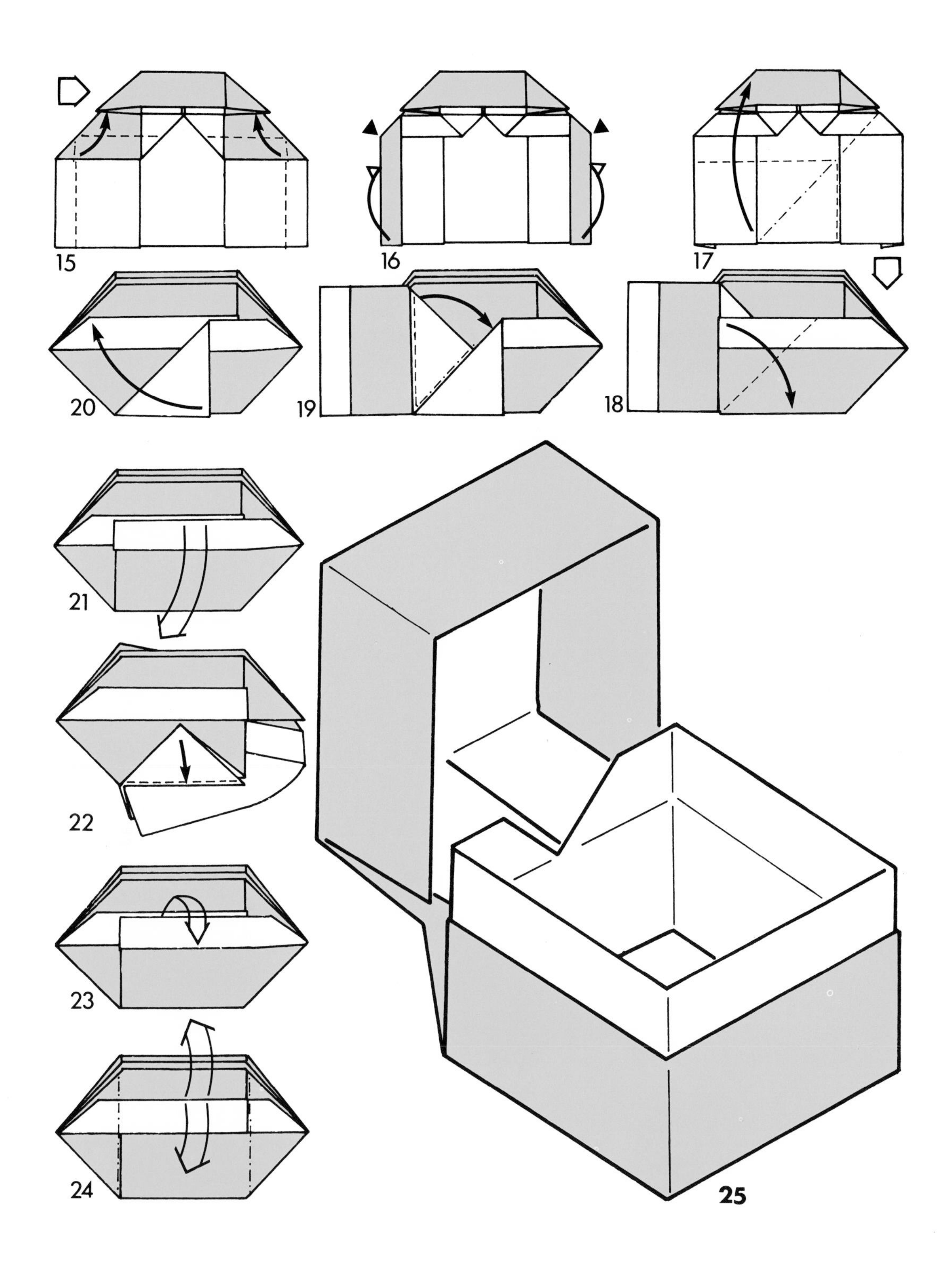

20 Return the front flap.

21 Pull the front edge down and . . .

22 . . . tuck the white triangular flap underneath the folded front edge – and close.

23 Bring the concealed raw edge to the front.

24 Raise and form the sides of the model . . .

25 . . . and see the completed box with lid emerge.

JEWEL (Toshie Takahama)

You will need three small squares of coloured paper, with sides about 3.5 cm (1.5 in) long, to make one jewel. Fold each square in the following way:

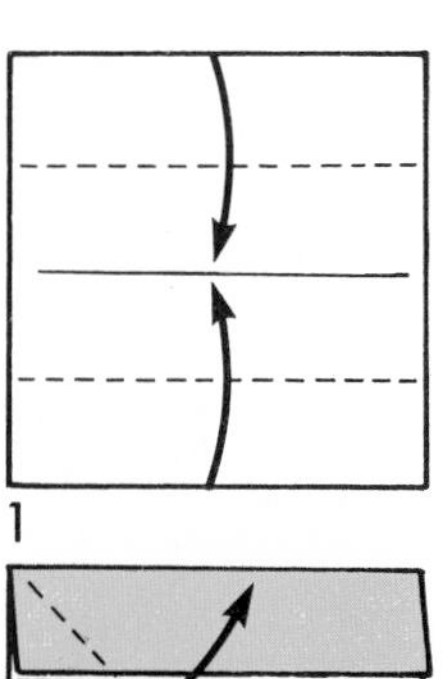

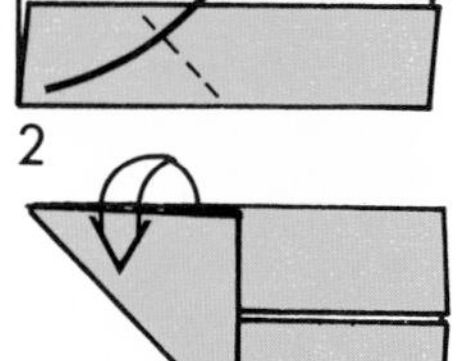

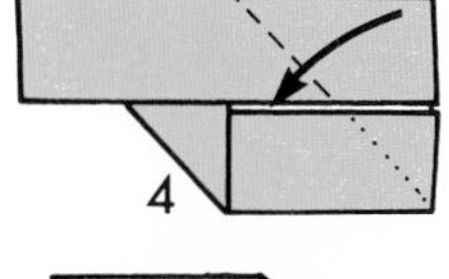

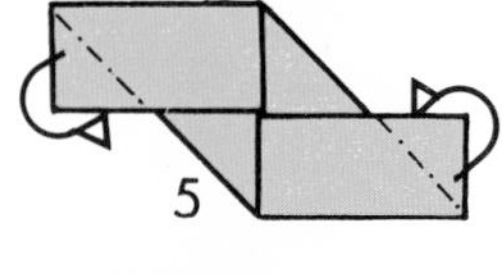

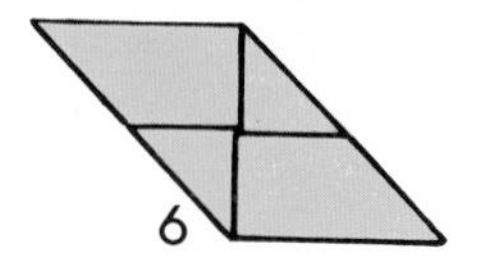

Starting with the white side up, first make the centre crease.

1 Fold top and bottom edges to centre.

2 Fold left edge to top.

3 Pull concealed flap to front.

4 Fold right edge to bottom, tucking point inside.

5 Mountain fold left and right corners behind.

6 This completes one unit.

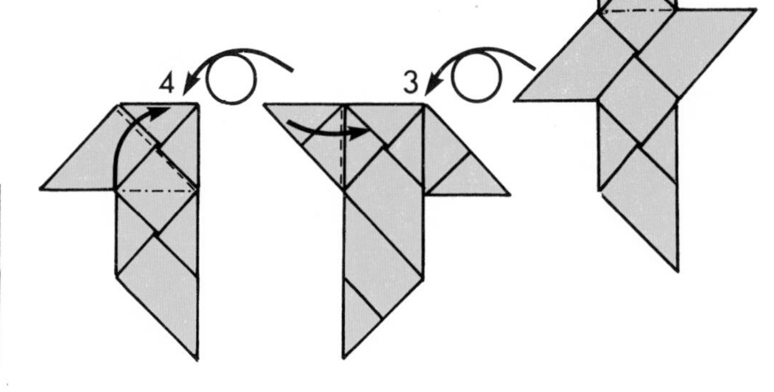

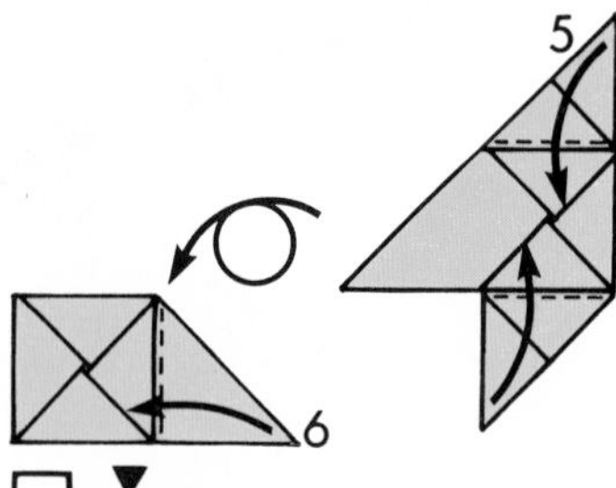

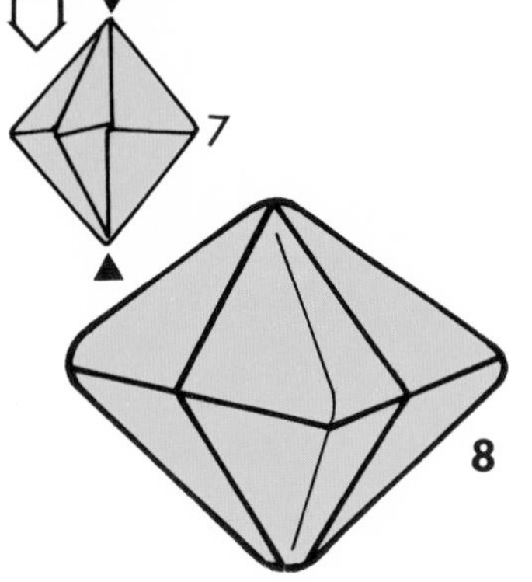

Assembling the jewel

1 Place the three units together like this, tucking the points into the centre pockets.

2 Mountain fold top point behind. Turn over.

3 Tuck left point into pocket. Turn over.

4 Swivel bottom point to left.

5 Tuck top and bottom points into pockets. Turn over.

6 Tuck right point into pocket.

7 Gently press top and bottom points between finger and thumb . . .

8 . . . and the jewel appears. Try threading about fifty jewels together to make a necklace.

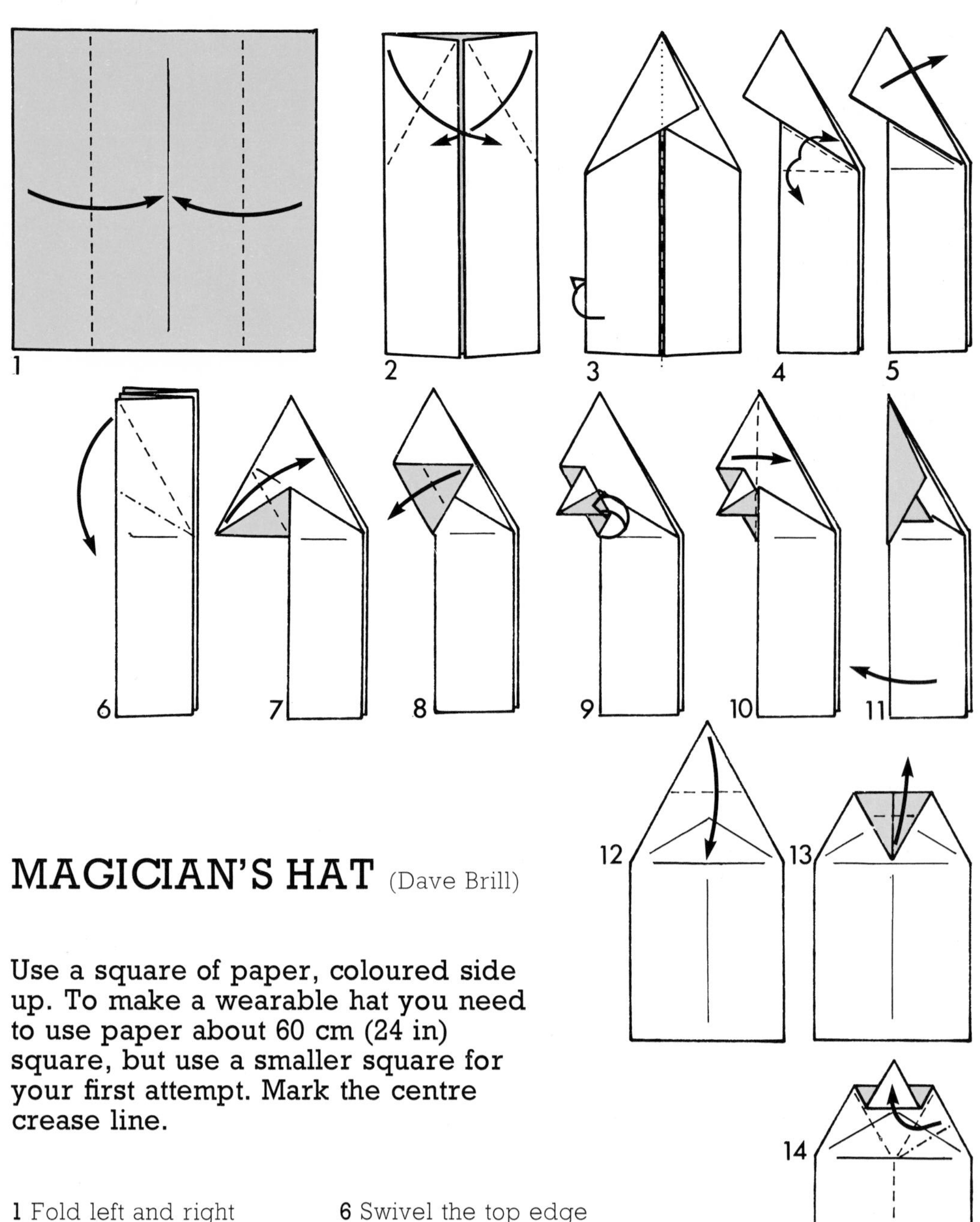

MAGICIAN'S HAT (Dave Brill)

Use a square of paper, coloured side up. To make a wearable hat you need to use paper about 60 cm (24 in) square, but use a smaller square for your first attempt. Mark the centre crease line.

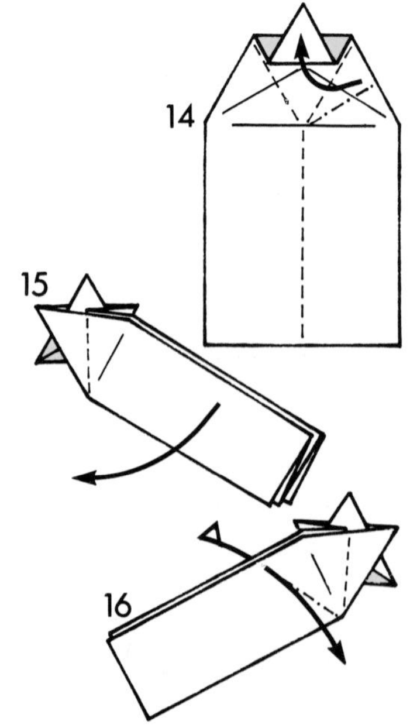

1 Fold left and right edges to centre.

2 Fold the top two corners down so that the outer edges meet on the vertical centre line.

3 Mountain fold in half.

4 Fold down over the folded edge; fold over again, crease firmly and return.

5 Raise the flap. Repeat behind.

6 Swivel the top edge down, using existing crease lines. Repeat behind.

7 Fold point to edge. Repeat behind.

8 Fold point outwards again (note that fold line passes through point where edges meet underneath). Repeat behind.

9 Bring raw edge to front. Repeat behind.

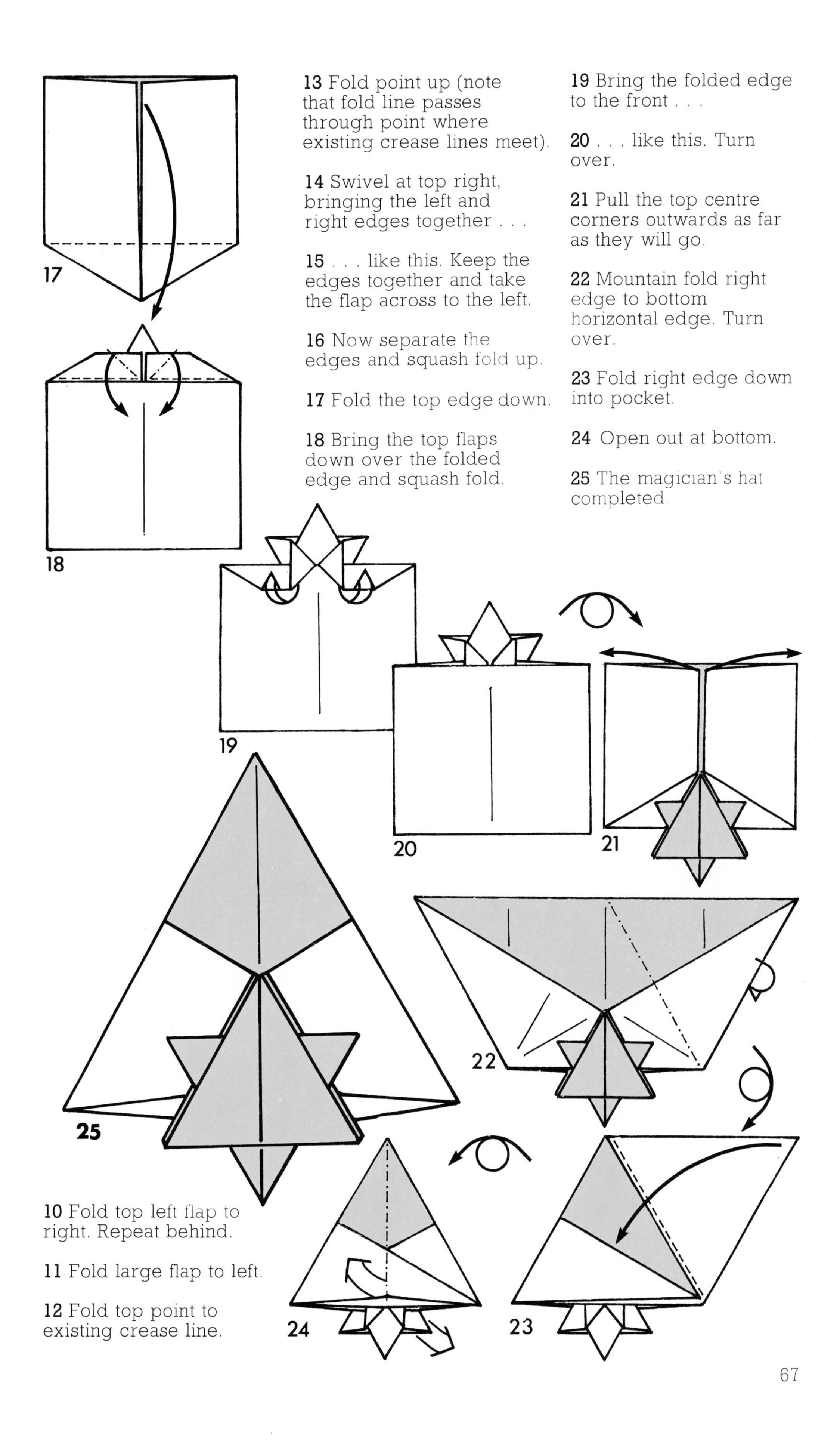

13 Fold point up (note that fold line passes through point where existing crease lines meet).

14 Swivel at top right, bringing the left and right edges together . . .

15 . . . like this. Keep the edges together and take the flap across to the left.

16 Now separate the edges and squash fold up.

17 Fold the top edge down.

18 Bring the top flaps down over the folded edge and squash fold.

19 Bring the folded edge to the front . . .

20 . . . like this. Turn over.

21 Pull the top centre corners outwards as far as they will go.

22 Mountain fold right edge to bottom horizontal edge. Turn over.

23 Fold right edge down into pocket.

24 Open out at bottom.

25 The magician's hat completed.

10 Fold top left flap to right. Repeat behind.

11 Fold large flap to left.

12 Fold top point to existing crease line.

MAGICIAN'S WAND (Dave Brill)

Use a 2 × 1 rectangle of fairly thin paper, white side up. Divide into sixths.

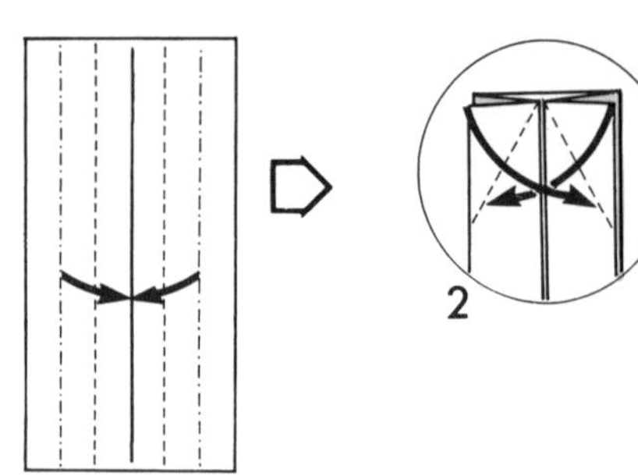

1 Pleat the outer creases to the centre line.

2 Fold the top two corners down so that the outer edges meet on the vertical centre line.

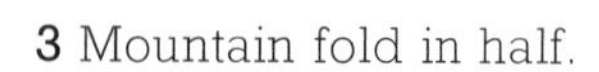

3 Mountain fold in half.

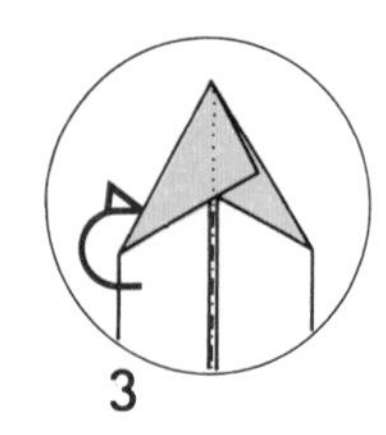

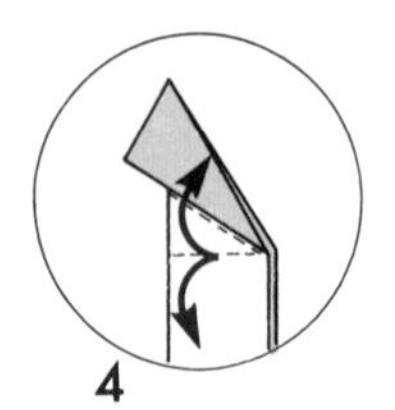

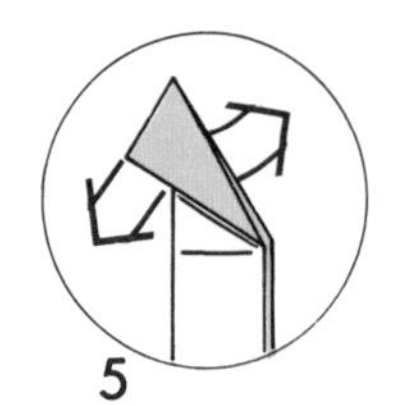

4 Fold down over the folded edge; fold over again, crease firmly and return.

5 Open up the paper completely.

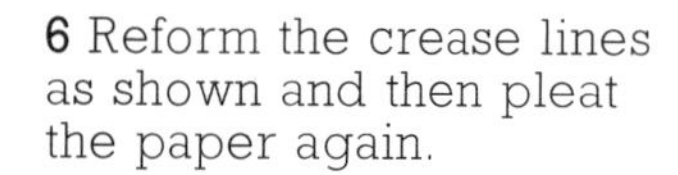

6 Reform the crease lines as shown and then pleat the paper again.

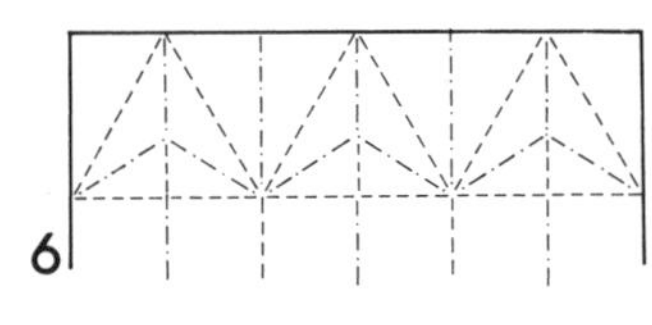

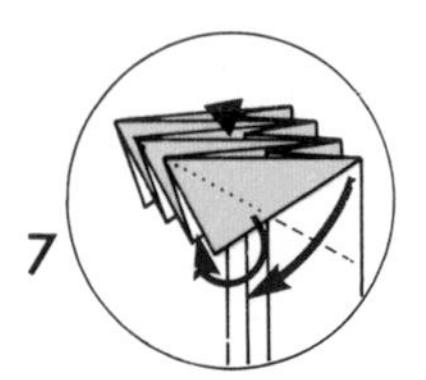

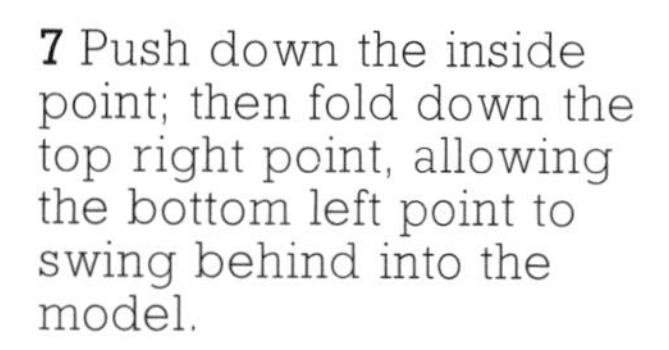

7 Push down the inside point; then fold down the top right point, allowing the bottom left point to swing behind into the model.

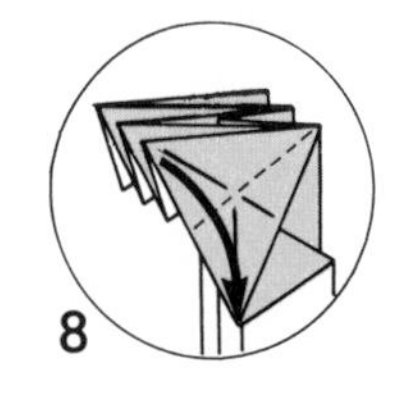

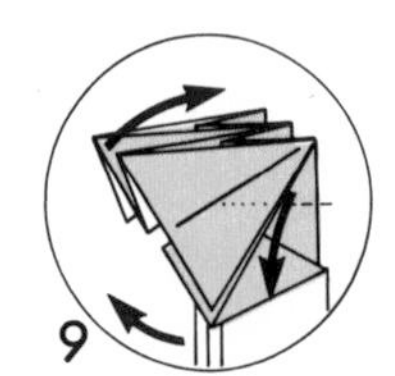

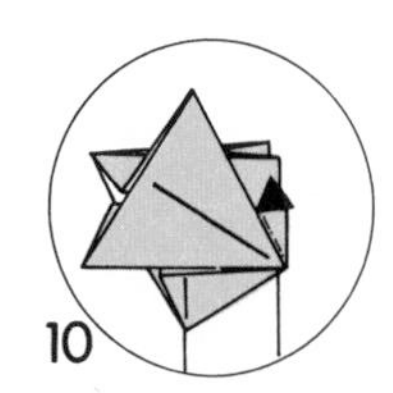

8 Fold down the top left point.

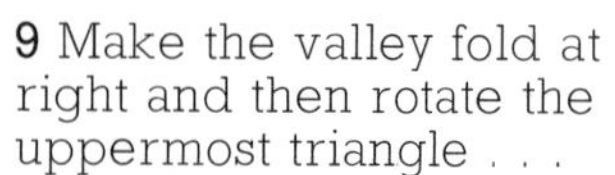

9 Make the valley fold at right and then rotate the uppermost triangle . . .

10 . . . to this position. Reverse fold at right. Turn over.

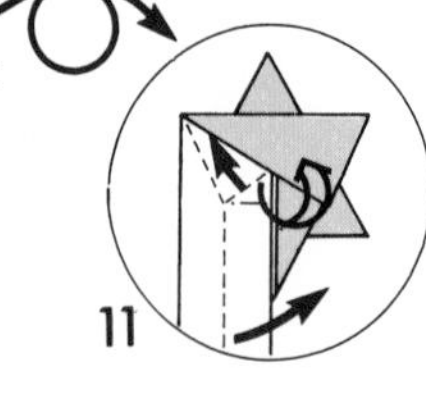

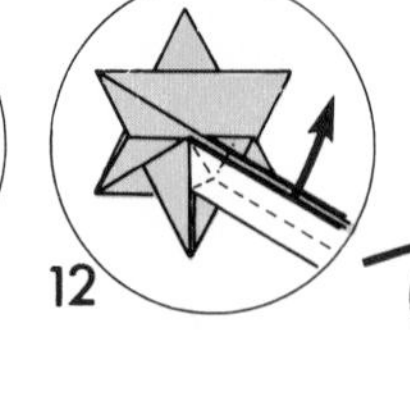

11 Pull concealed edge to front at right. Fold the vertical edges of the white strip together and swing it to the right.

12 Narrow the white strip again in the same way. Turn over.

13 The magician's wand completed.

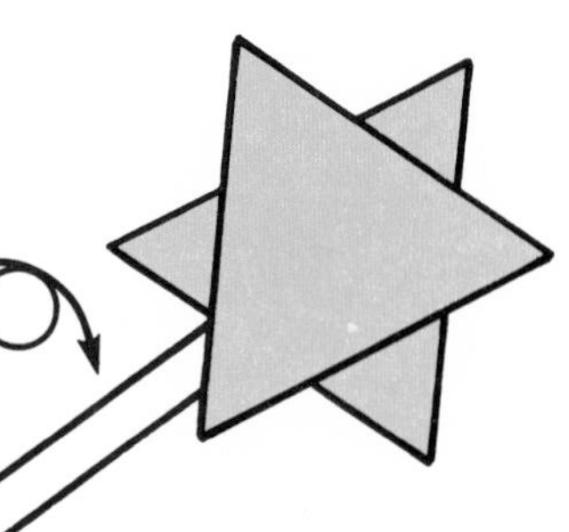

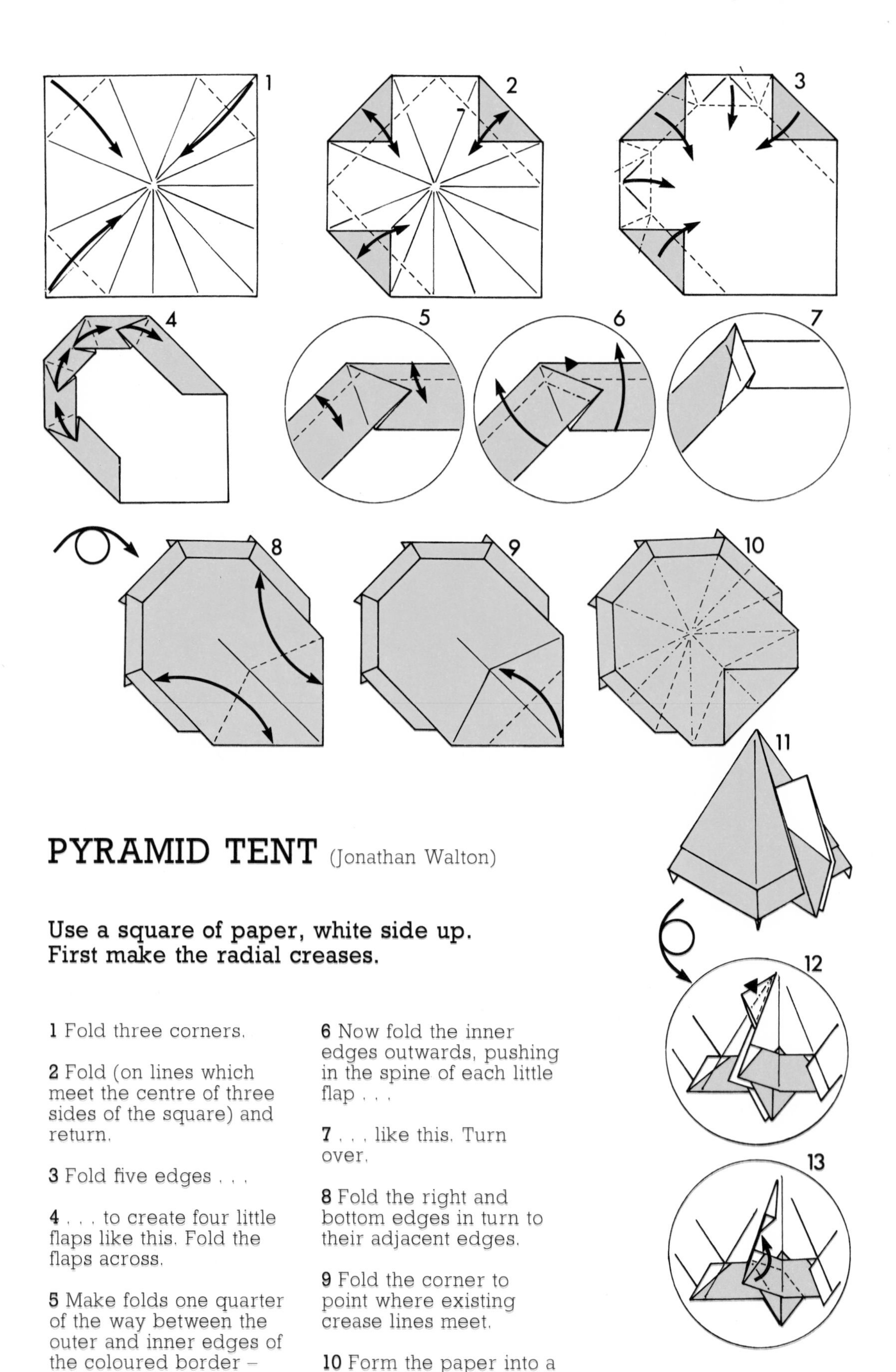

PYRAMID TENT (Jonathan Walton)

Use a square of paper, white side up. First make the radial creases.

1 Fold three corners.

2 Fold (on lines which meet the centre of three sides of the square) and return.

3 Fold five edges . . .

4 . . . to create four little flaps like this. Fold the flaps across.

5 Make folds one quarter of the way between the outer and inner edges of the coloured border – and return.

6 Now fold the inner edges outwards, pushing in the spine of each little flap . . .

7 . . . like this. Turn over.

8 Fold the right and bottom edges in turn to their adjacent edges.

9 Fold the corner to point where existing crease lines meet.

10 Form the paper into a pyramid shape . . .

11 . . . like this. Turn over and look inside model.

12 Squash fold the little flap, taking sides over edges of larger flap (to help hold the two surfaces together).

13 Swivel the bottom edge up. Repeat at left.

14 Swivel the white triangular area forward. Do *not* repeat at left.

15 Push surplus paper underneath folded edge . . .

16 . . . like this. Turn over.

17 Mountain fold uppermost flap of entrance pocket.

18 Fold lower flap up into model. Turn upside down.

19 Fold large inside flap (to help hold model together). Form entrance pocket into tunnel shape.

20 Detail of gusset at each corner: spread sides apart and flatten . . .

21 . . . like this. The border has now moved into horizontal plane. Turn right way up.

22 The pyramid tent completed.

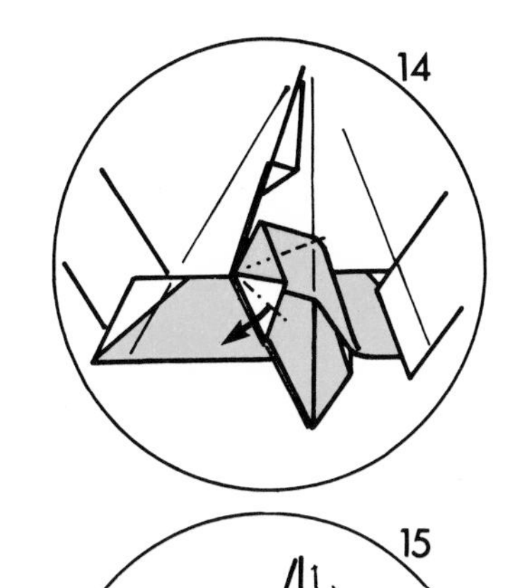

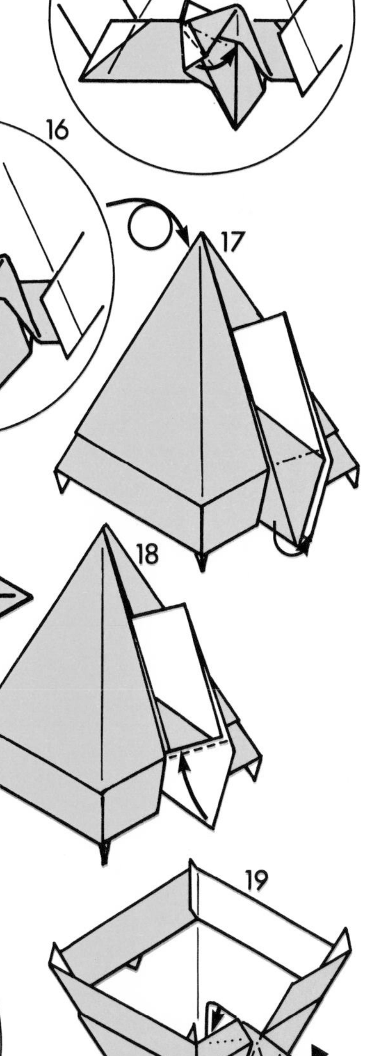

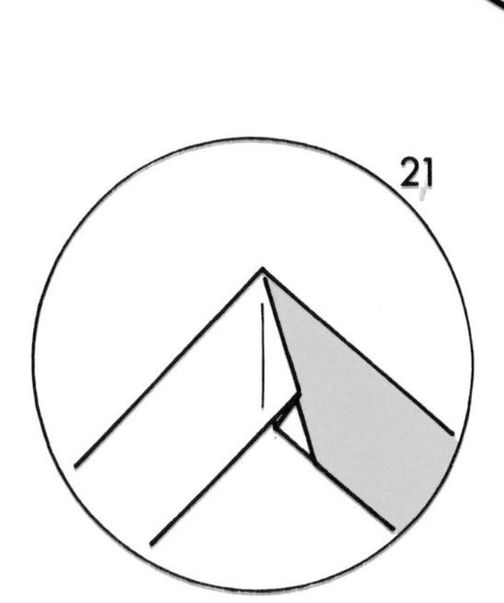

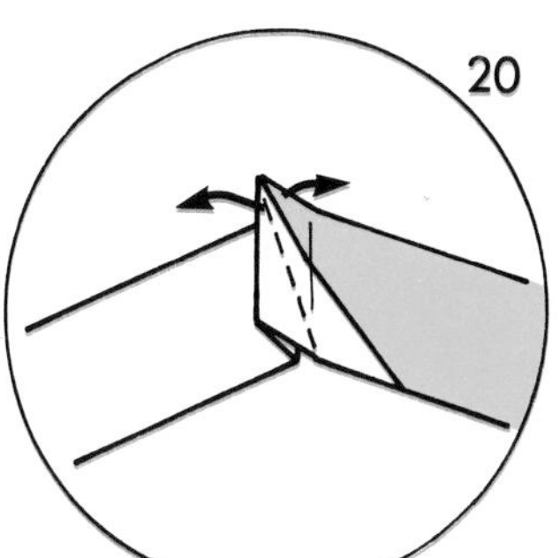

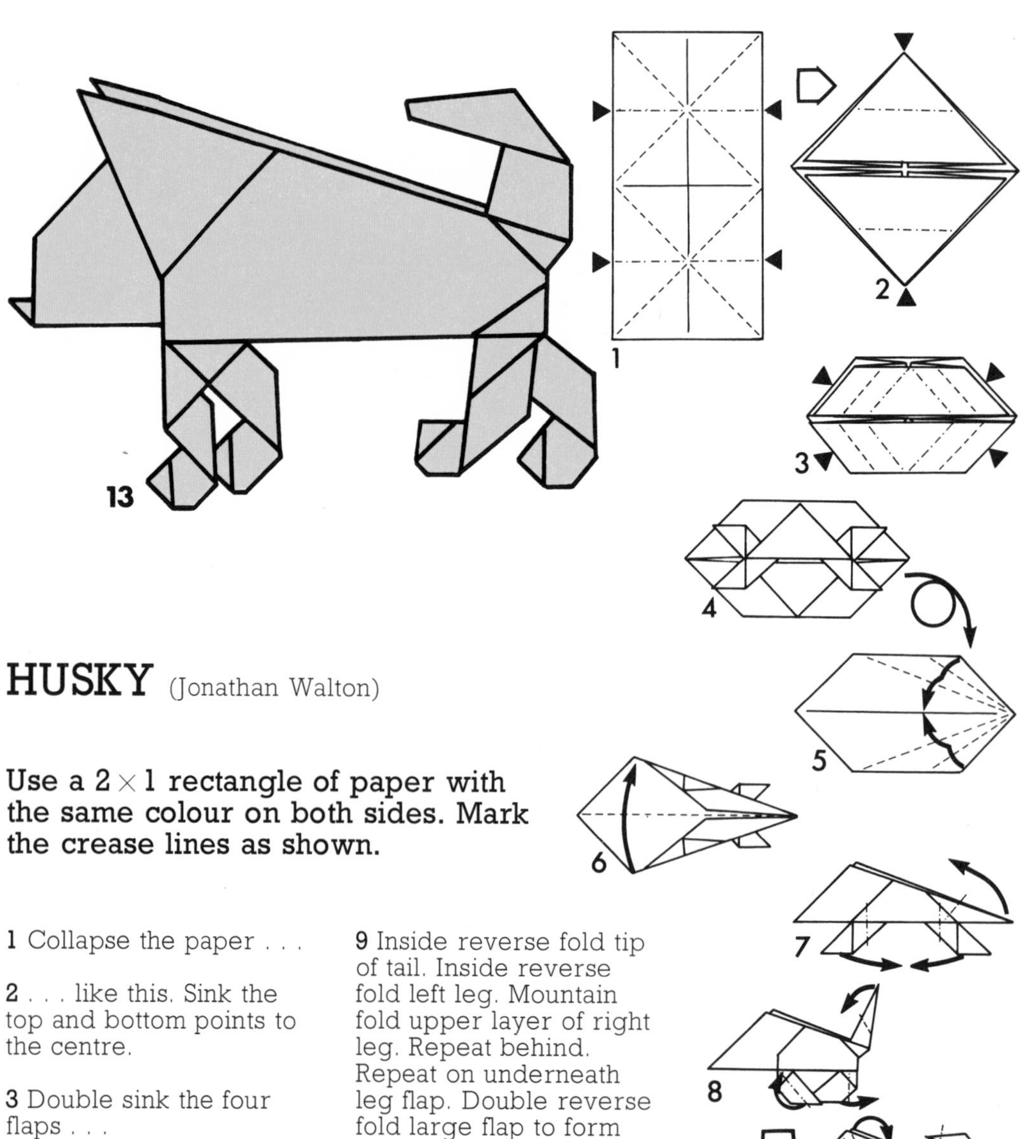

HUSKY (Jonathan Walton)

Use a 2 × 1 rectangle of paper with the same colour on both sides. Mark the crease lines as shown.

1 Collapse the paper . . .

2 . . . like this. Sink the top and bottom points to the centre.

3 Double sink the four flaps . . .

4 . . . like this. Turn over.

5 Fold the right edges over twice to the horizontal centre line.

6 Fold model in half.

7 Inside reverse fold tail at right. Inside reverse fold leg flaps. Repeat behind.

8 Outside reverse fold tail. Inside reverse fold leg flap at right. Repeat behind. Mountain fold upper layer of left leg flap into model. Repeat behind. Then repeat on underneath leg flap.

9 Inside reverse fold tip of tail. Inside reverse fold left leg. Mountain fold upper layer of right leg. Repeat behind. Repeat on underneath leg flap. Double reverse fold large flap to form head.

10 Inside reverse fold left leg. Crimp right leg. Mountain fold edge of head into model; repeat behind and crimp point inside to form nose.

11 Double reverse fold head. Inside reverse fold all four legs.

12 Outside reverse fold four leg points to form paws.

13 The completed husky. Try making a team of huskies to go with the 'Nansen' sledge on page 74.

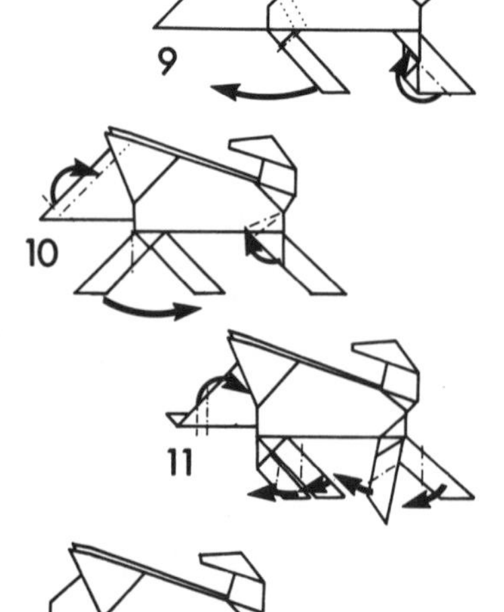

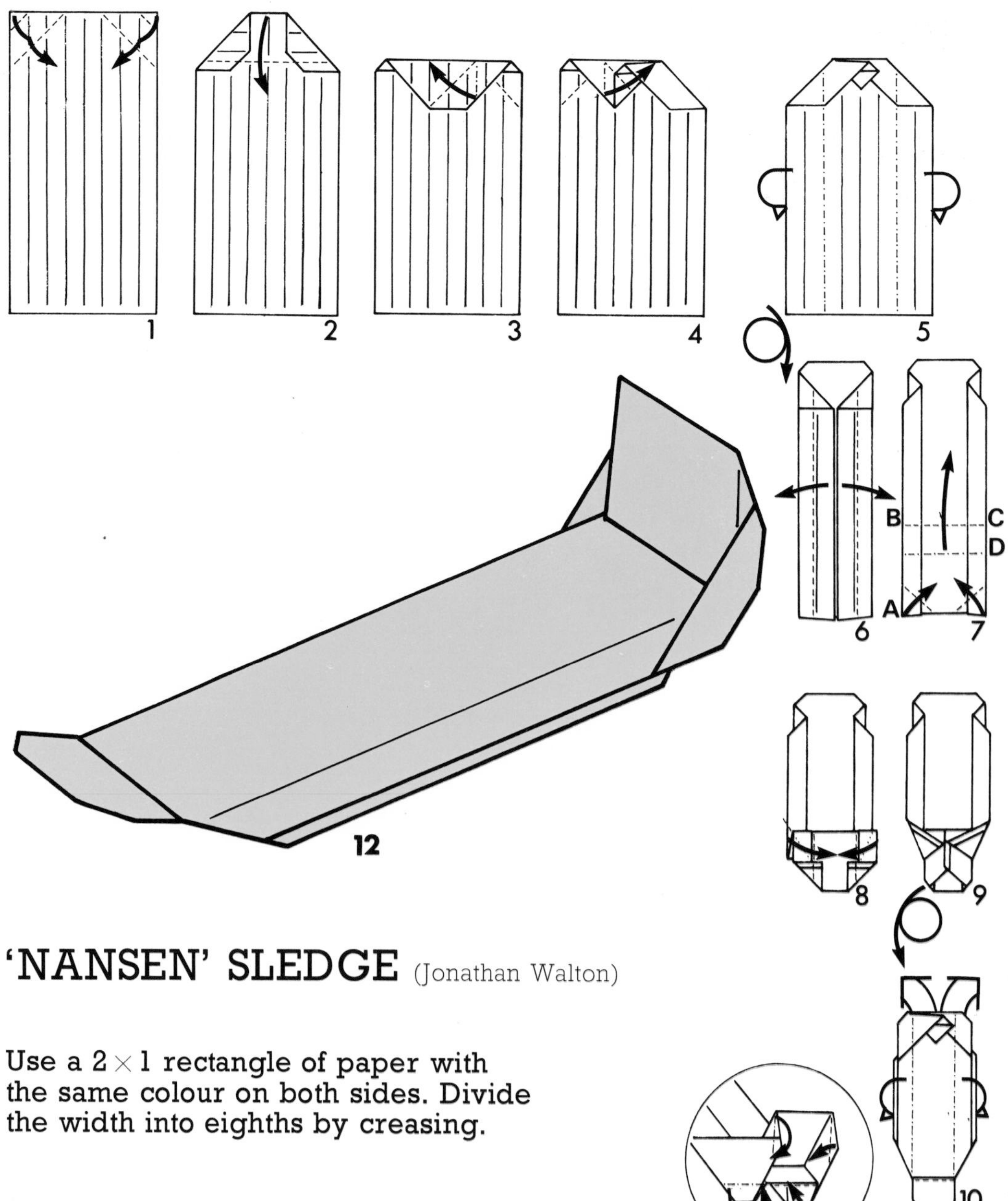

'NANSEN' SLEDGE (Jonathan Walton)

Use a 2 × 1 rectangle of paper with the same colour on both sides. Divide the width into eighths by creasing.

1 Fold each top corner down to the one-eighth line, then fold over to the three-eighths line.

2 Fold top edge down; note that the fold line lies between two existing crease lines.

3 Swivel right diagonal edge to top; here, too, the axis lies between two crease lines.

4 Swivel left diagonal edge to top.

5 Mountain fold edges to centre behind. Turn over.

6 Fold centre edges to left and right so that they slightly overlap outer edges.

7 First fold bottom corners, then pleat (AB = BC and CD = one third of AB).

8 Take the top two layers of the pleat to the vertical centre line, squashing behind . . .

9 . . . like this. Turn over.

10 Mountain fold sides 90° behind; paper at top will open to form back of sledge.

11 Shape back of sledge.

12 The 'Nansen' sledge completed.

CHIMPANZEE (John Richardson)

Use a square of paper, coloured side up. Make the vertical centre crease, then find the horizontal eighth line at bottom.

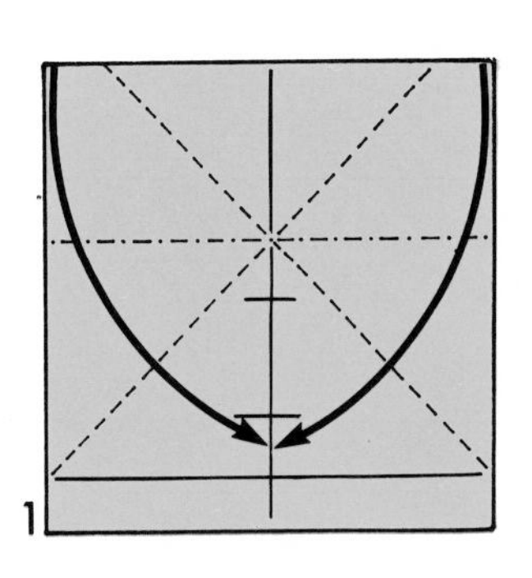

1 Make the folds as shown, then collapse the paper . . .

2 . . . like this. Fold top point to point X (which lies a quarter of the way between points A and B) and return.

3 Now fold again, but only the upper layer this time. Separate the two layers by putting fingers into the model at the sides and flatten the top point.

4 Step 3 in progress.

5 Step 3 completed. Inside reverse fold side flaps.

6 Take hold of raw edge inside model and pull to bottom . . .

7 . . . like this. Push in sides of panel and raise flap in new plane.

8 Separate vertical edges and squash fold.

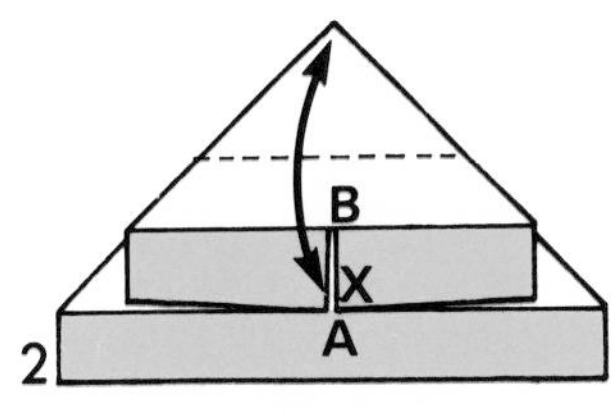

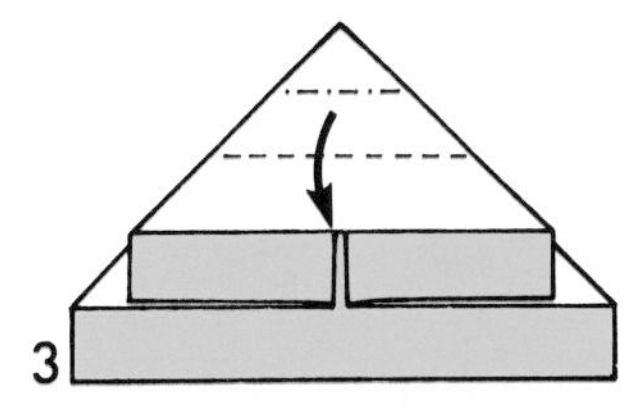

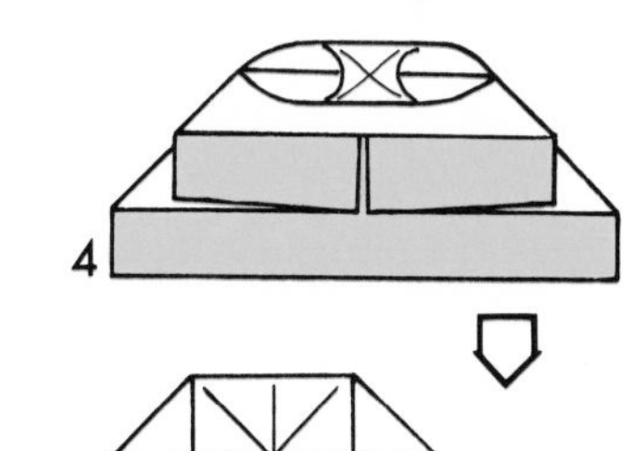

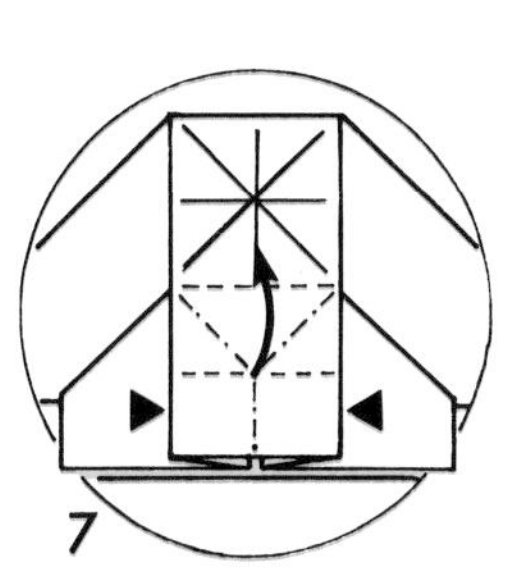

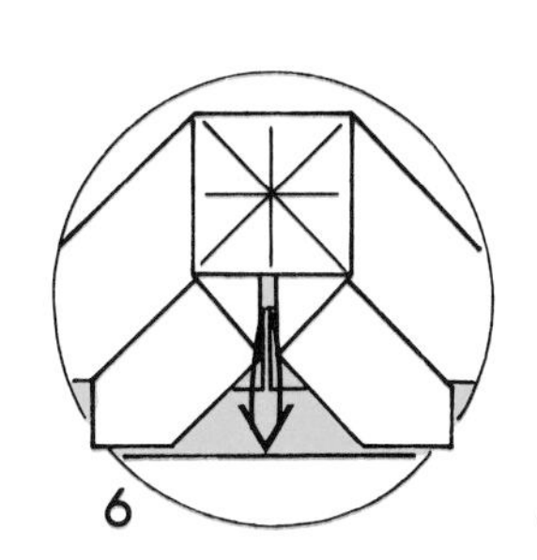

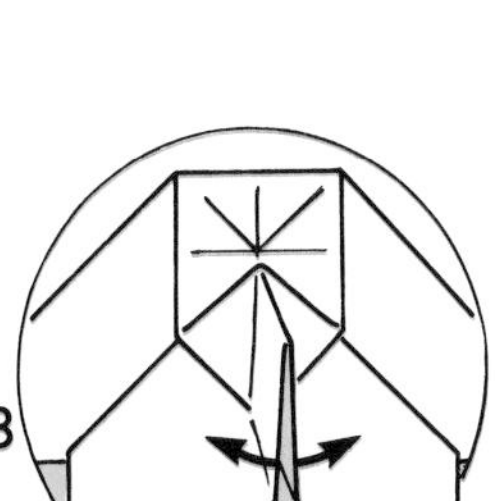

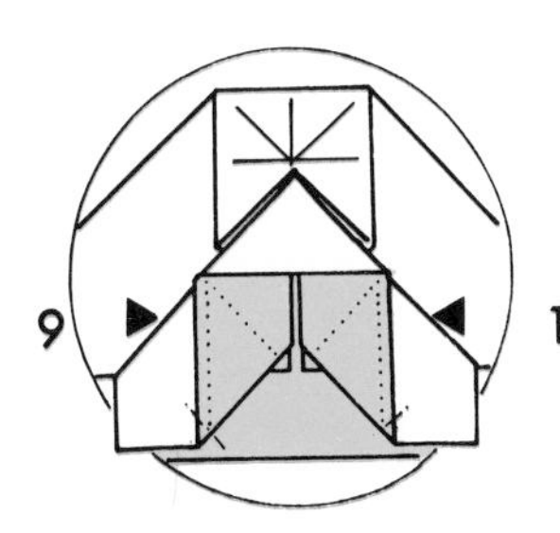

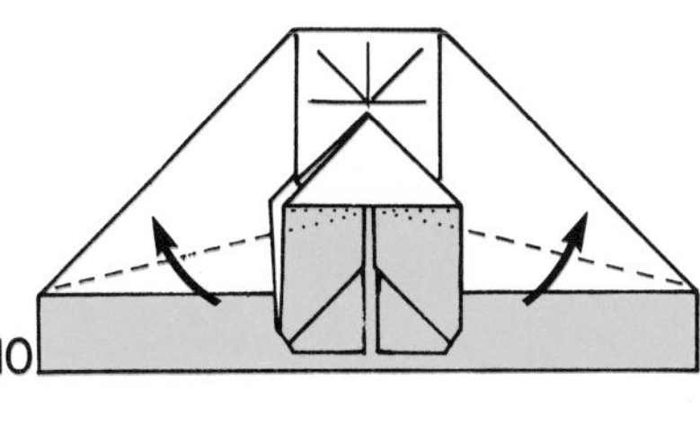

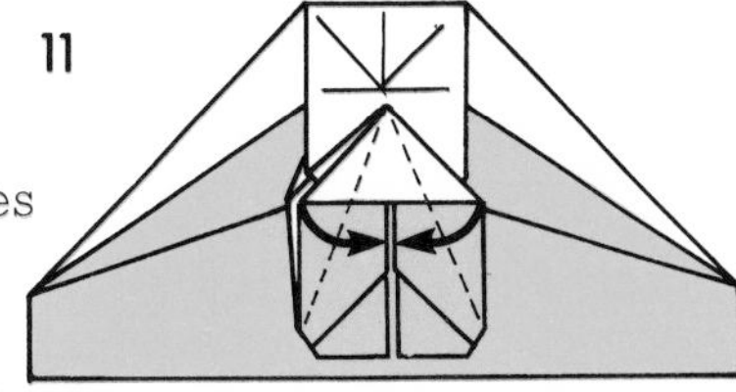

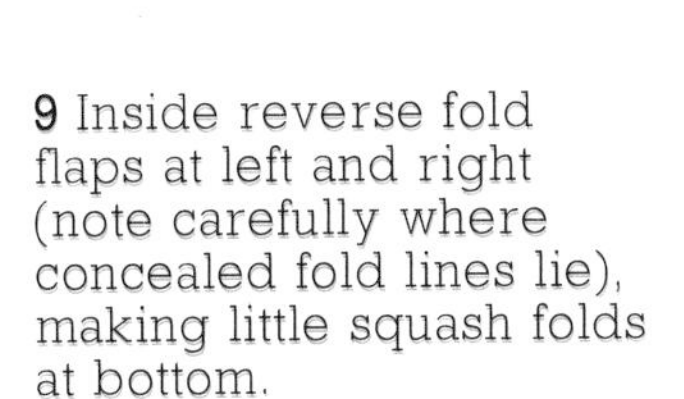

9 Inside reverse fold flaps at left and right (note carefully where concealed fold lines lie), making little squash folds at bottom.

10 Fold horizontal edges up, swivelling paper behind centre flap.

11 Fold corners of centre flap.

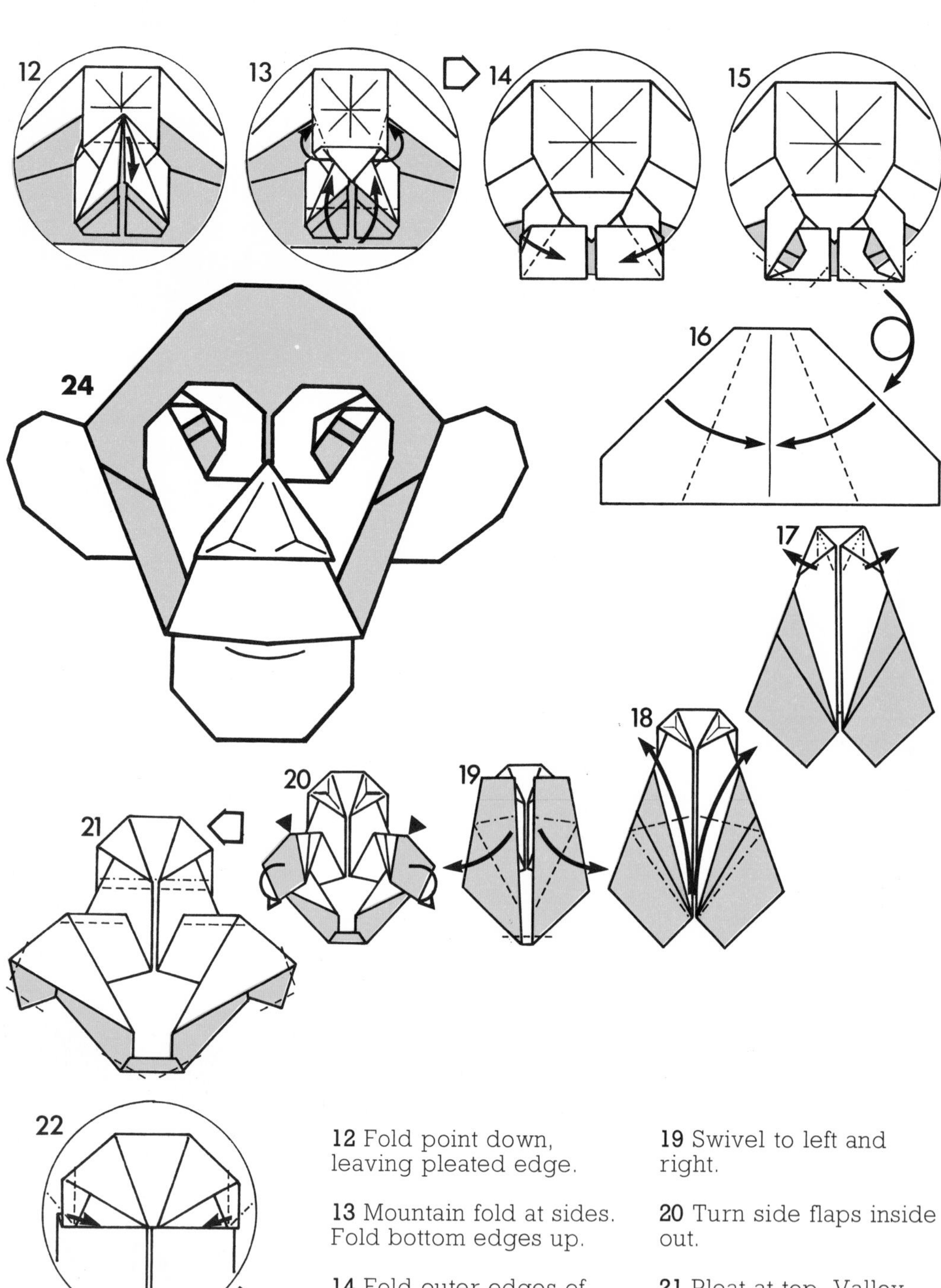

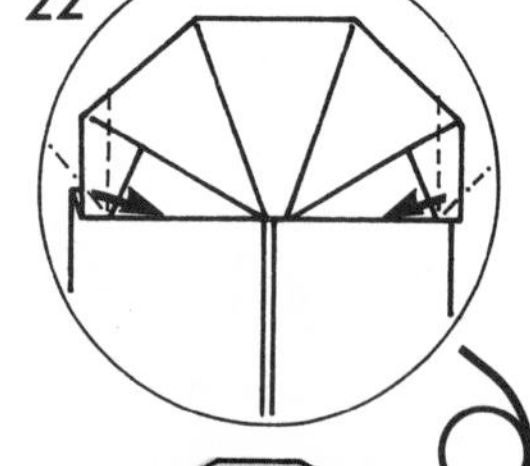

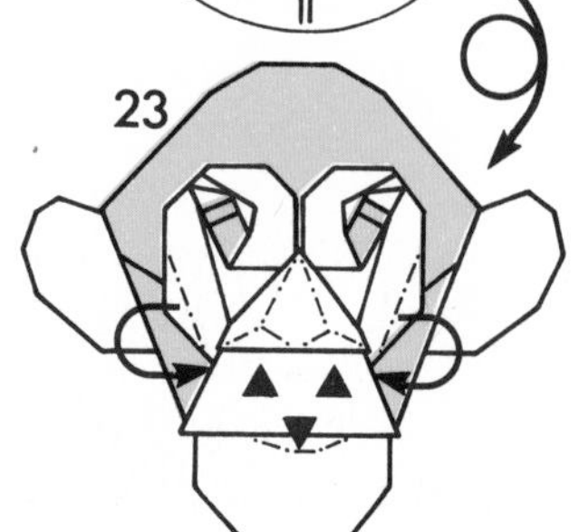

12 Fold point down, leaving pleated edge.

13 Mountain fold at sides. Fold bottom edges up.

14 Fold outer edges of two bottom flaps.

15 Mountain fold four bottom corners. Turn over.

16 Fold diagonal edges to centre crease.

17 Swivel at top, flattening points.

18 Swivel bottom points up.

19 Swivel to left and right.

20 Turn side flaps inside out.

21 Pleat at top. Valley fold other corners and edges.

22 Swivel vertical edges at either side of the pleat. Turn over and rotate.

23 Mountain fold cheeks. Shape nose and mouth.

24 The chimpanzee completed.

THREE-MASTED SAILING SHIP (Martin Wall)

Use a large (at least 25 cm or 10 in) square of thin, strong paper. Complete steps 1–3 of the flower vase on page 22 and rotate it so that the raw edges are at the bottom.

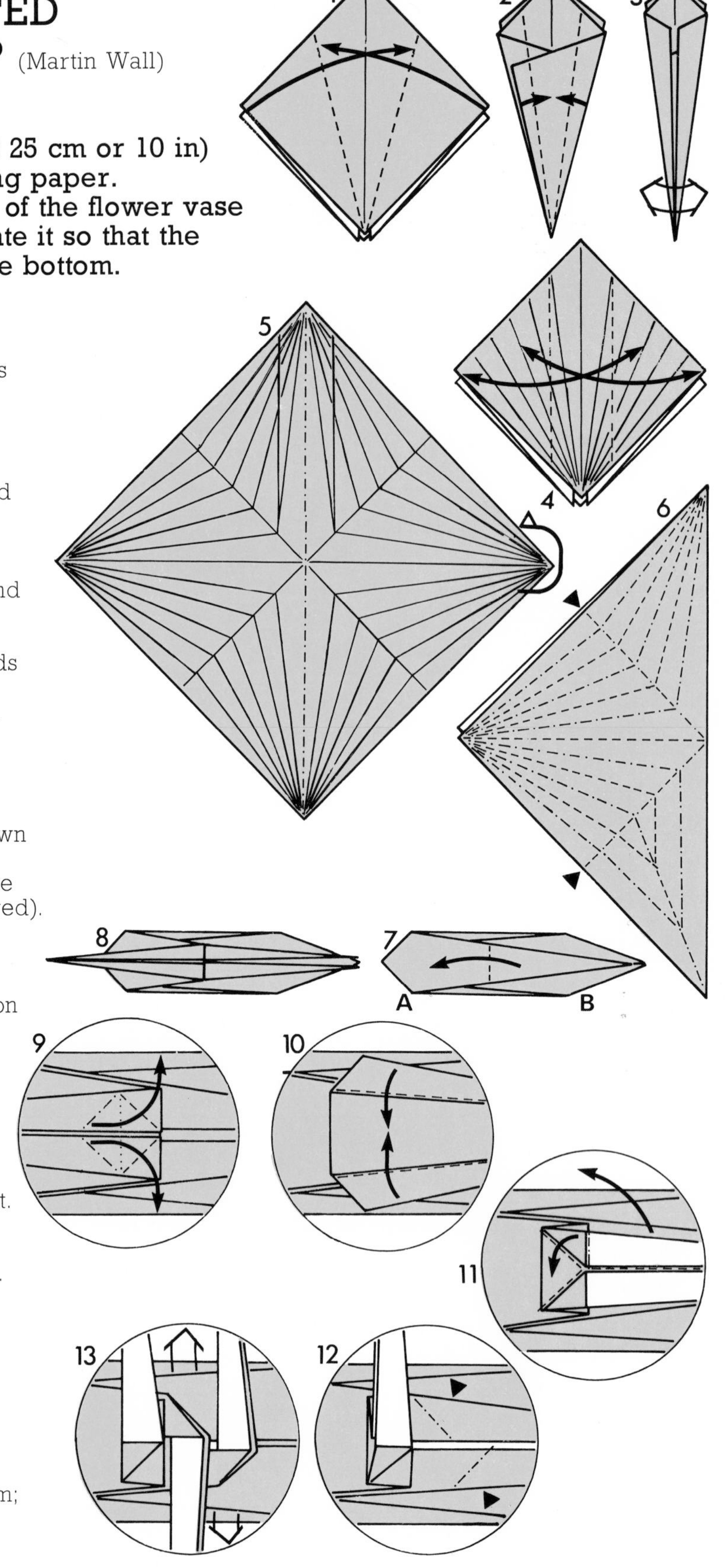

1 Fold the bottom edges at a 30° angle . . .

2 . . . so that the folded edges cross on the vertical centre line. Fold left and right edges to centre. Repeat behind.

3 Open up the paper and return to fig. 1.

4 Make two vertical folds (which meet existing crease lines at top) and return. Open up.

5 Mountain fold in half.

6 Make all folds as shown and repeat behind (most, but not all, crease lines have been prepared). Collapse the paper . . .

7 . . . into this shape. Fold upper flap to left on line halfway between points A and B.

8 Step 7 completed.

9 Separate the raw edges at centre and squash fold flap to right.

10 Fold raw edges of flap over folded edges.

11 Rabbit-ear fold flap up.

12 Inside reverse fold next two flaps.

13 Pull out concealed paper at top and bottom; turn base of sail flaps inside out . . .

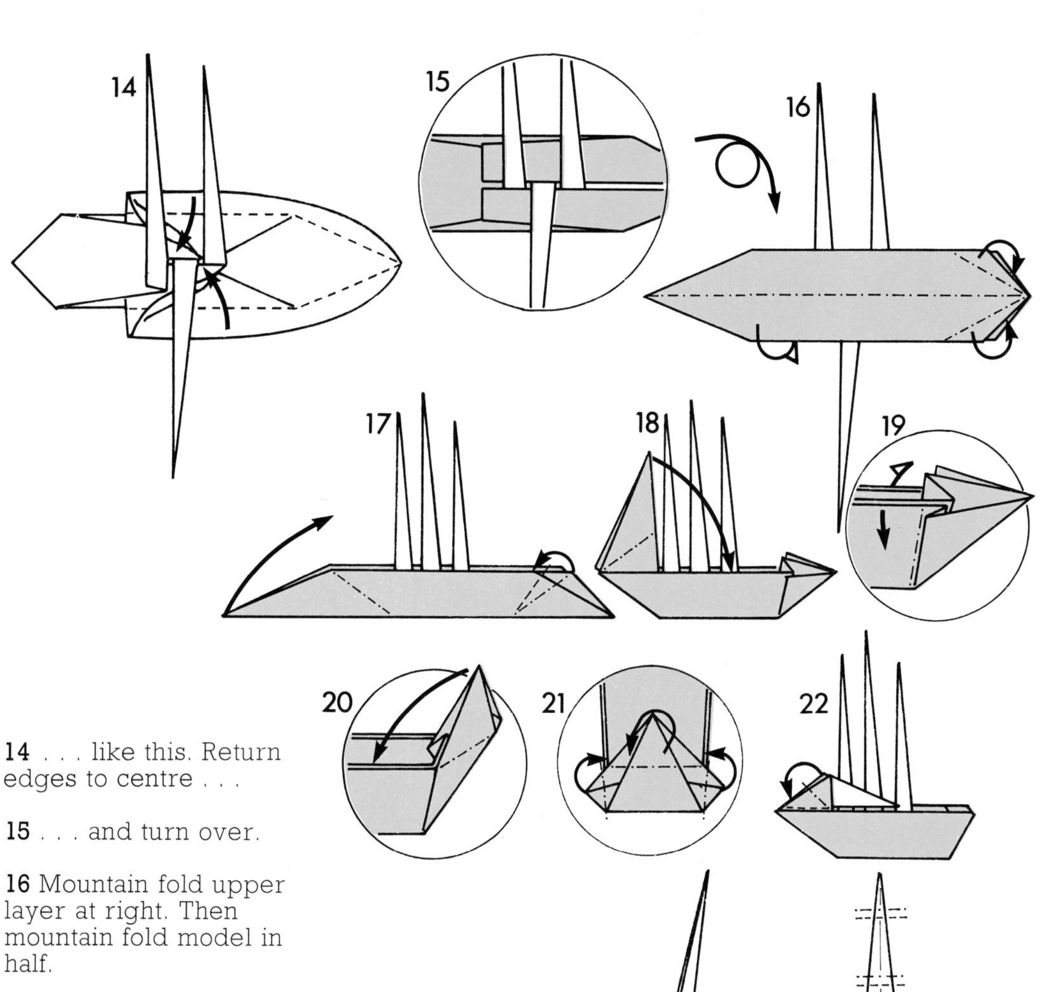

14 . . . like this. Return edges to centre . . .

15 . . . and turn over.

16 Mountain fold upper layer at right. Then mountain fold model in half.

17 Inside reverse fold at left. Crimp at right.

18 Inside reverse fold at left to expose white side.

19 Separate upper and lower layers at right to form rear of ship.

20 Fold flap into horizontal plane.

21 Top view: fold centre point down into model. Tuck side points into pockets.

22 Crimp.

23 Bring under layer to front. Repeat behind.

24 Separate the two layers of the mainsail, flattening at bottom. Repeat on other two sails.

25 Front view: pleat the mainsail. Repeat on other two sails. Gently curve all sails.

26 The three-masted sailing ship completed.

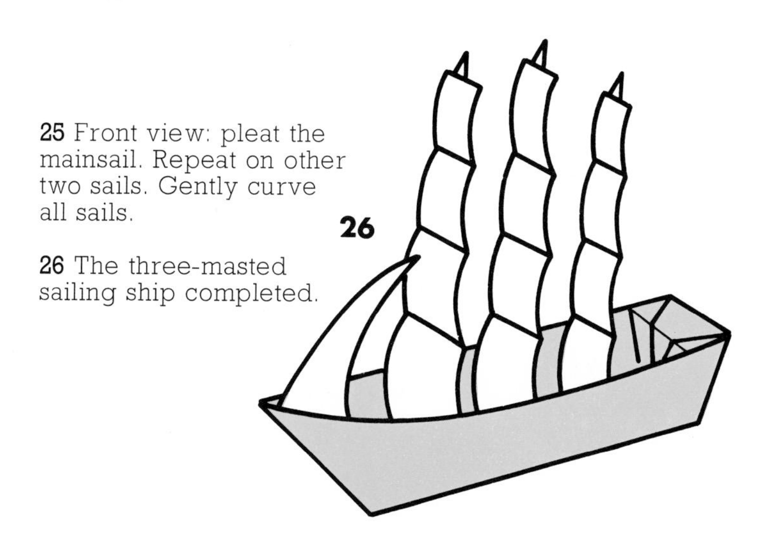

SEAGULL (Laurie Bisman)

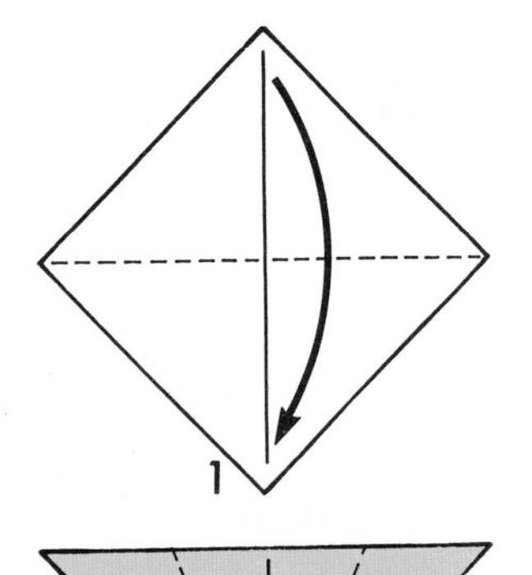

Use a square of coloured paper, white side up. Mark the centre crease.

1 Fold the top point to bottom.

2 Fold the diagonal edges to the centre crease.

3 Mountain fold top points over folded edge.

4 Open paper out to fig. 2.

5 Fold bottom point up.

6 Swivel top diagonal edges to centre line.

7 Fold in half.

8 Inside reverse fold at top. Outside reverse fold at bottom.

9 Inside reverse fold at left. Outside reverse fold at right.

10 Outside reverse fold at left to form head. Crimp at right to form tail.

11 Double reverse fold to form beak.

12 The completed seagull. This is another 'flapping bird', like the one on page 40. Hold the bird's breast and pull his tail to make the wings move.

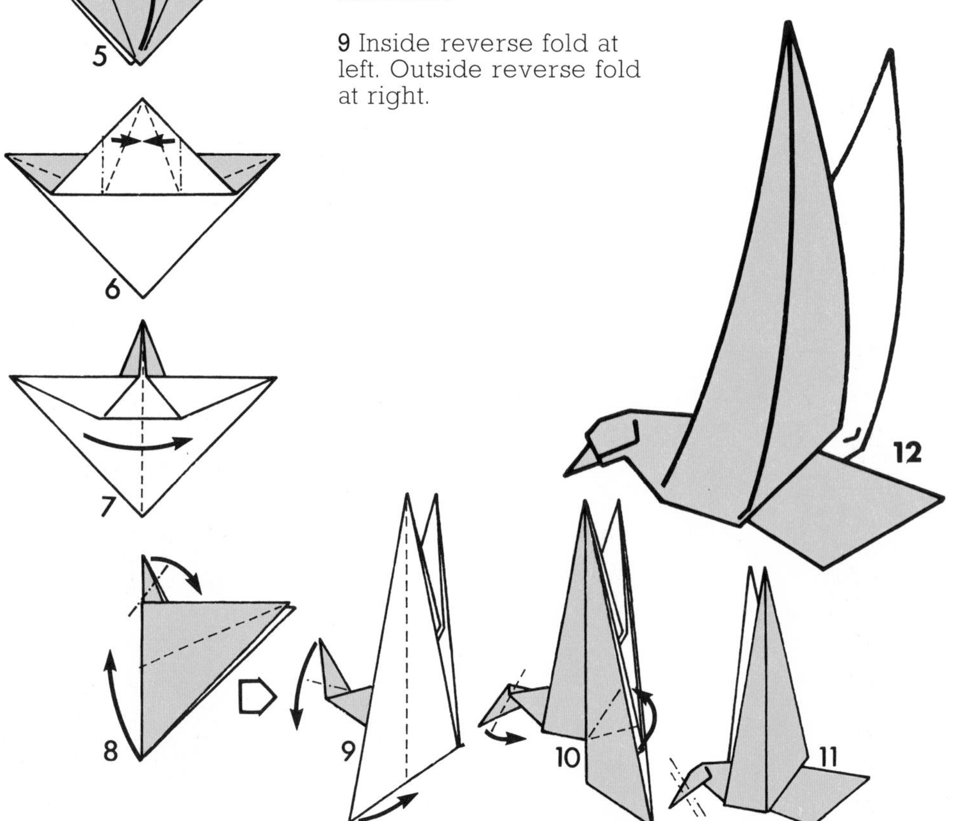

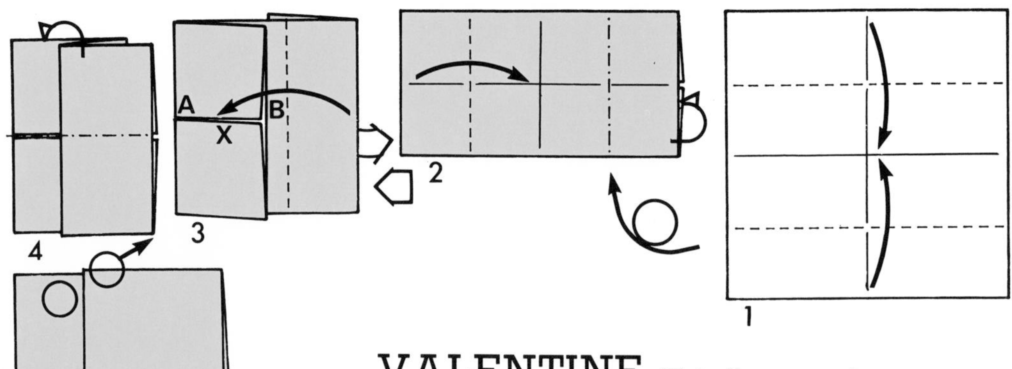

VALENTINE (Eric Kenneway)

Use a square of red paper, white side up. Mark the centre creases.

1 Fold top and bottom edges to the centre. Turn over.

2 Fold left edge to centre. Mountain fold right edge to centre behind.

3 Fold right edge to point X (which lies halfway between points A and B). Let the concealed edge kick out to right.

4 Mountain fold in half.

5 Hold at top left and pull the two folded edges apart . . .

6 . . . like this. Press firmly so that paper will hold new shape. Inside reverse fold at left, right and centre. Repeat centre reverse fold behind.

7 Mountain fold bottom point into the model. Repeat behind.

8 Swivel the diagonal edge to right. Repeat behind. Rotate paper through 180°.

9 Mountain fold top point into the model. Repeat behind. Tuck right point into pocket.

10 Form two heart shapes.

11 The valentine completed.

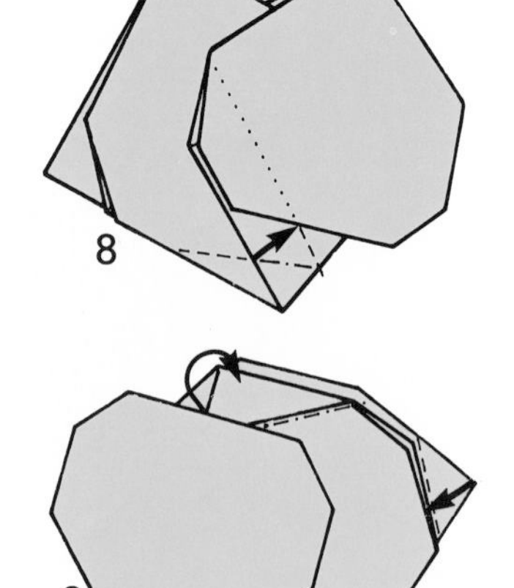

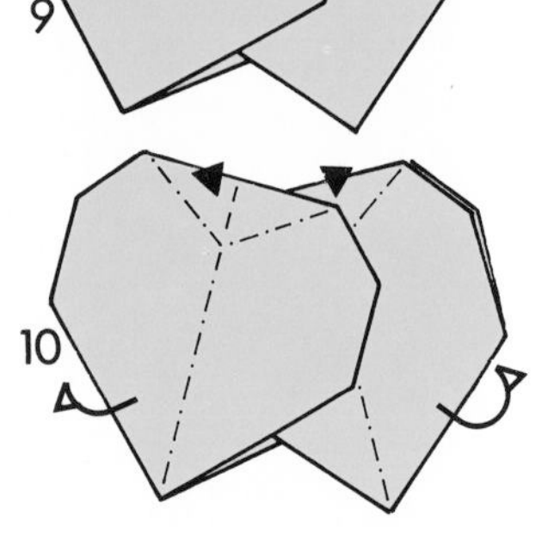

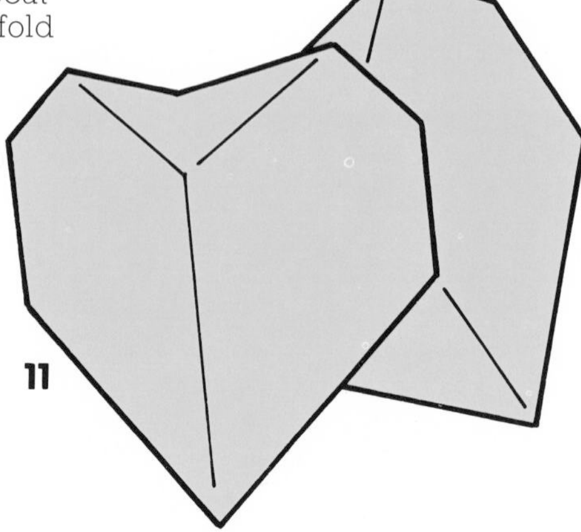

STAR (Eric Kenneway)

Prepare a hexagon of coloured paper, white side up.

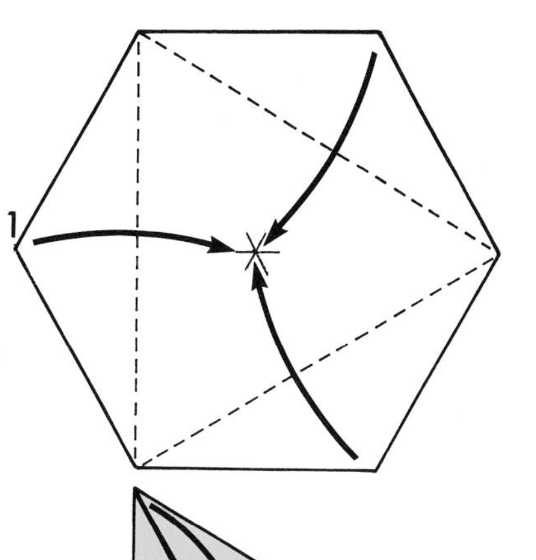

1 Fold three alternate corners to the centre.

2 Fold remaining three corners to the centre.

3 Pull out concealed raw edges.

4 Fold alternate raw edges . . .

5 . . . like this. Turn over.

6 Fold one edge to centre.

7 Fold adjacent edge to centre, swivelling point across . . .

8 . . . and again . . .

9 . . . and again . . .

10 . . . and again.

11 Swivel remaining point and . . .

12 . . . pull concealed point to top.

13 Fold this point down.

14 Pull out concealed point from each of six sides.

15 The star completed.

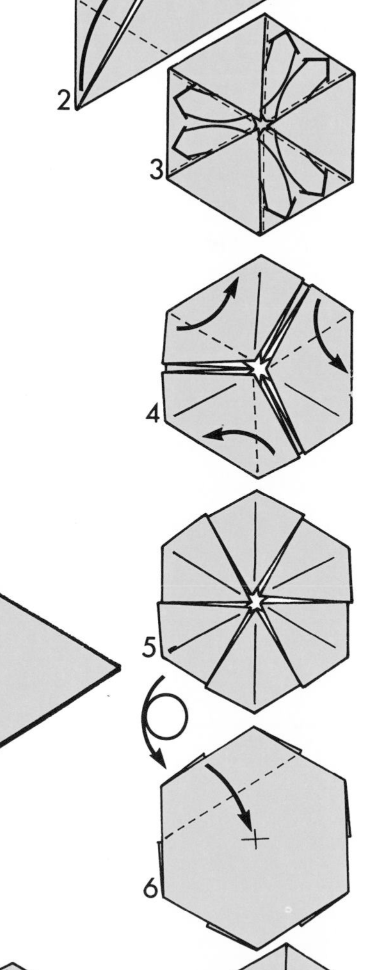

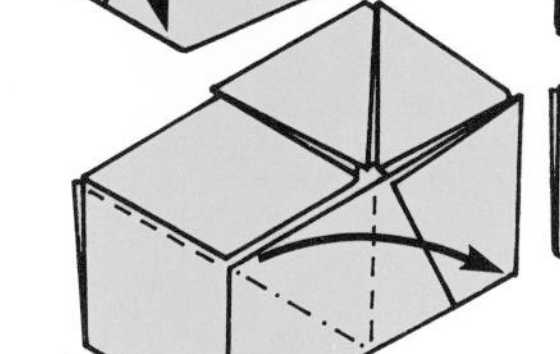

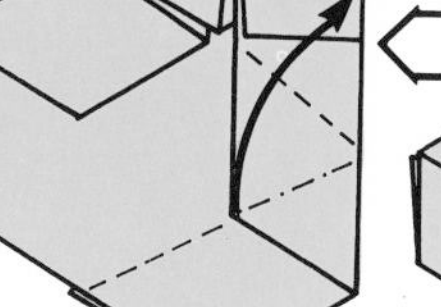

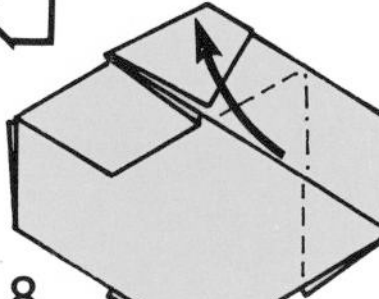

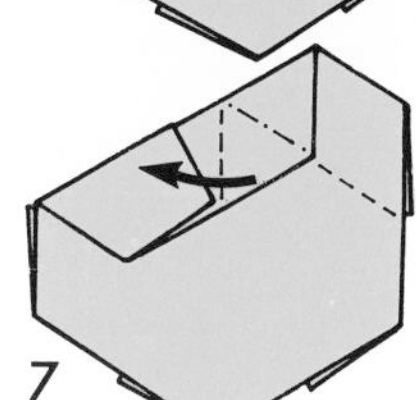

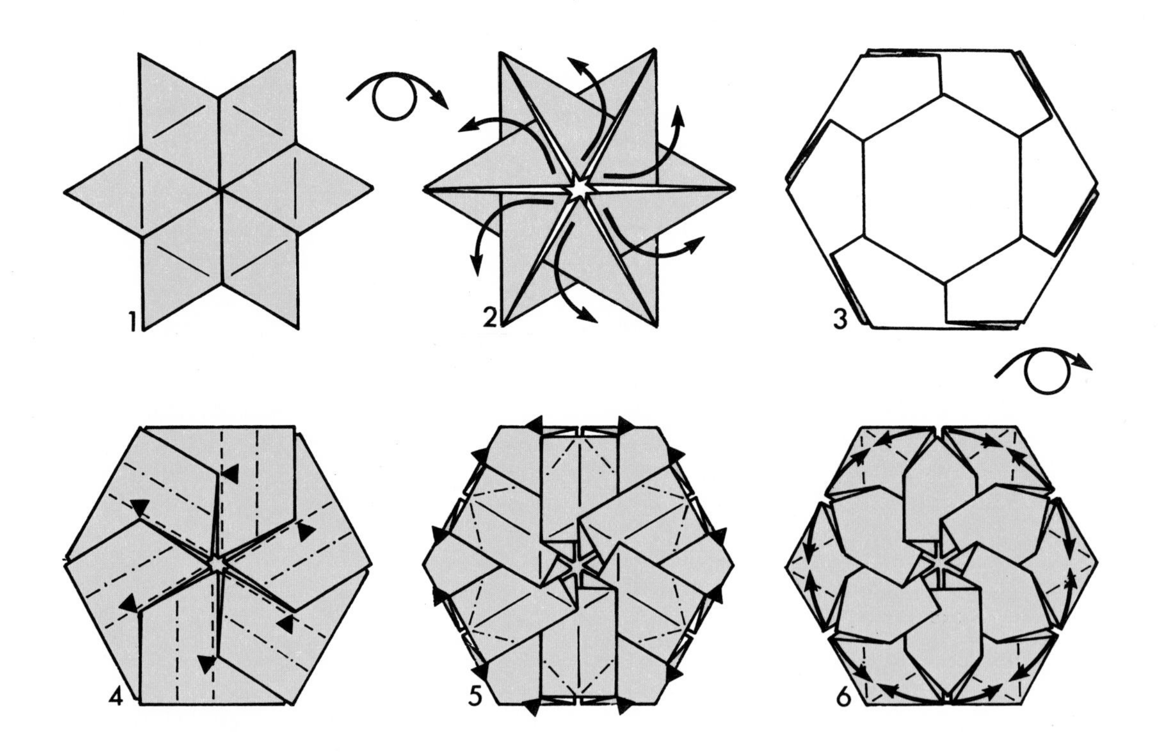

FLOWER DECORATION

(Eric Kenneway)

Use a hexagon of coloured paper and complete the star on page 83.

1 Turn over.

2 Pull the raw edges outwards from the centre . . .

3 . . . like this. Turn over.

4 Raise each flap in turn and flatten.

5 Inside reverse fold the outer corners of each rectangular flap.

6 Inside reverse fold the sides of each outer flap to its centre.

7 The flower decoration completed. See if you can develop the star into other decorative shapes.

HEDGEHOG (John Richardson)

Prepare a large 2 × 3 rectangle of brown wrapping paper. Divide the width into eighteenths and the length into twenty-sevenths; making crease lines.

1 Fold top, bottom and right edges inwards on second crease line from edge. At left, fold edge to first crease line; then fold on line halfway between second and third crease.

2 At each corner pull out concealed paper . . .

3 . . . into a point like this. Turn paper over.

4 Study the fold lines carefully (note that some lie on existing crease lines and some halfway between crease lines); then make eight pleats.

5 Now make horizontal pleats. Swivel leg flaps under at right.

6 Fold the two leg flaps to right. Repeat behind. Mountain fold overlapping square at right diagonally in half; then fold remaining seven squares similarly. Repeat behind.

7 Starting at right, raise concealed pleated edge into a reverse fold; then raise next pleated edge similarly. Continue until 48 reverse folds have been raised . . .

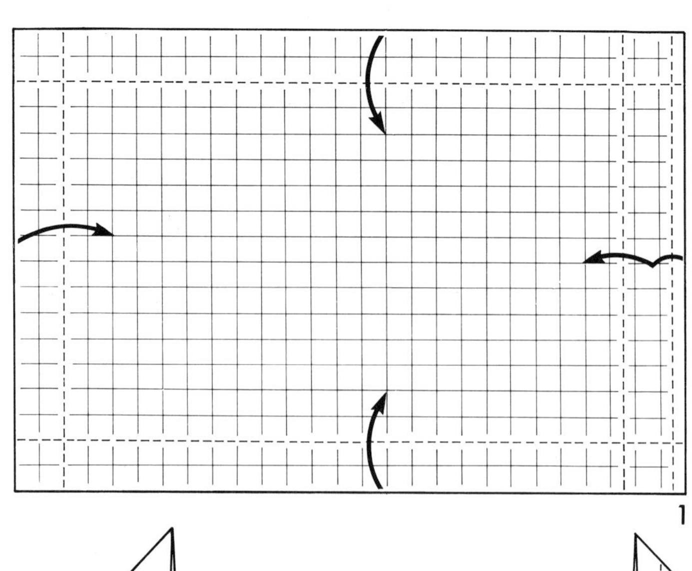

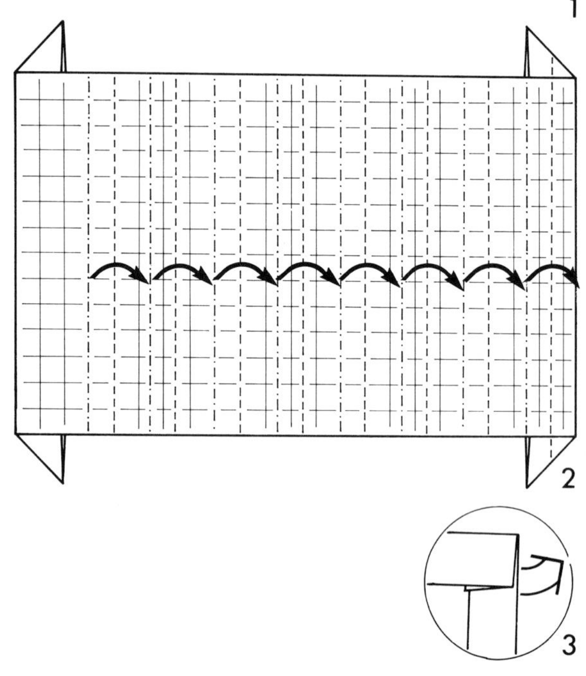

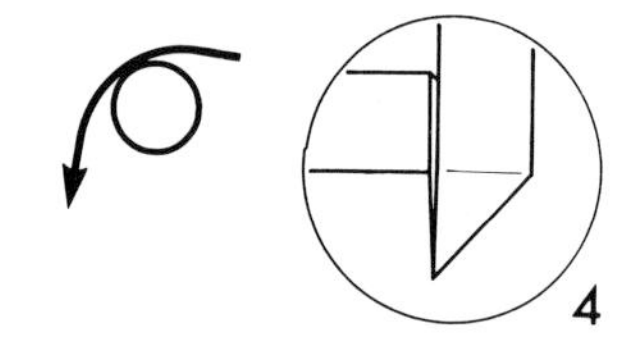

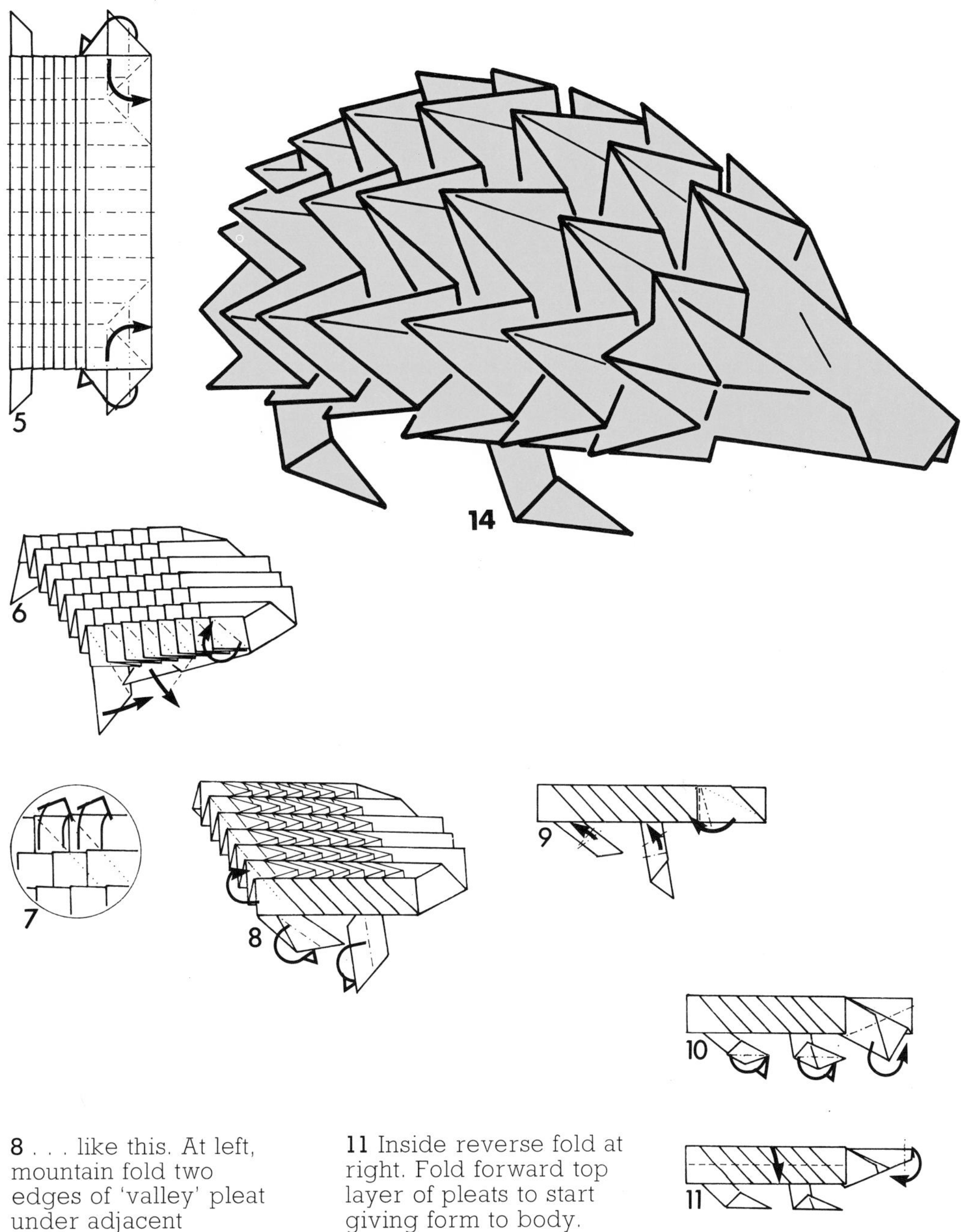

8 . . . like this. At left, mountain fold two edges of 'valley' pleat under adjacent 'mountain' pleat diagonally. Fold remaining five valley pleats similarly. Mountain fold leg flaps in half. Repeat behind.

9 Swivel legs. Repeat behind. Swivel at right. Repeat behind.

10 Mountain fold feet. Repeat behind. Mountain fold at right. Repeat behind.

11 Inside reverse fold at right. Fold forward top layer of pleats to start giving form to body. Repeat behind.

12 Slightly flatten nose at right.

13 Continue to shape the body: hold the ridge of one pleat and pull up a point from it; and continue until all 49 points are raised and the body appears rounded.

14 The hedgehog completed.

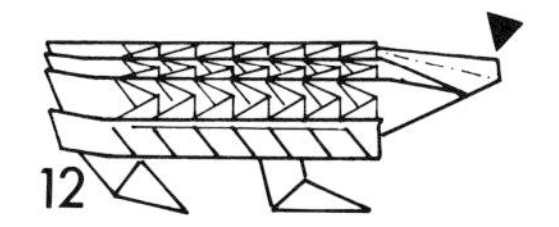

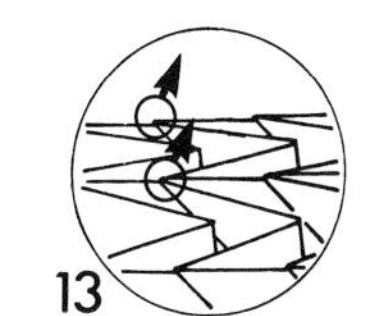

13

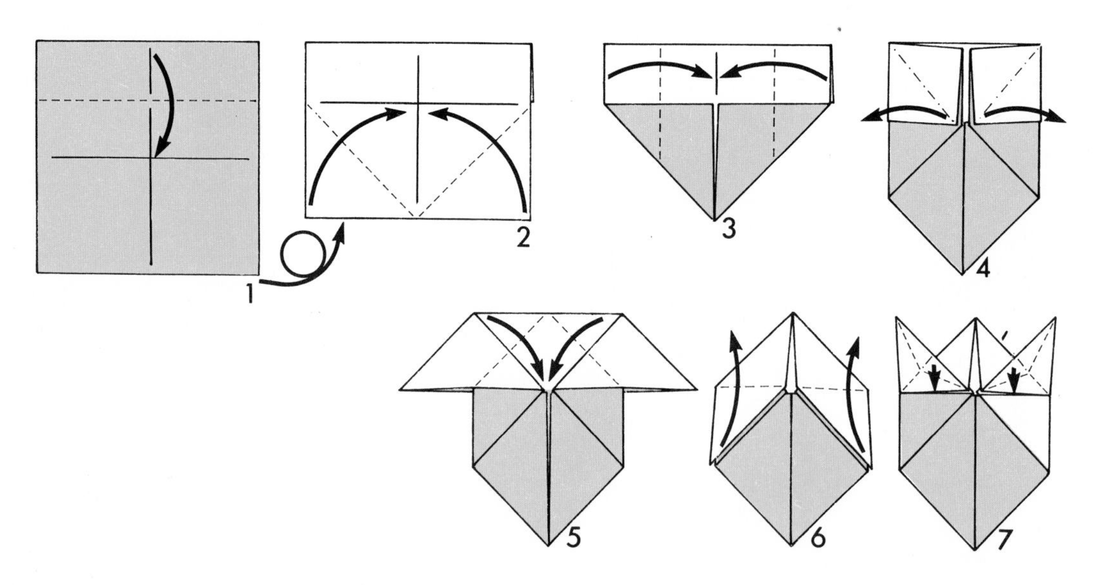

LADYBIRD (Hiroshi Kumasaka)

Use a very small square of spotted, red paper, coloured side up. Mark the centre creases.

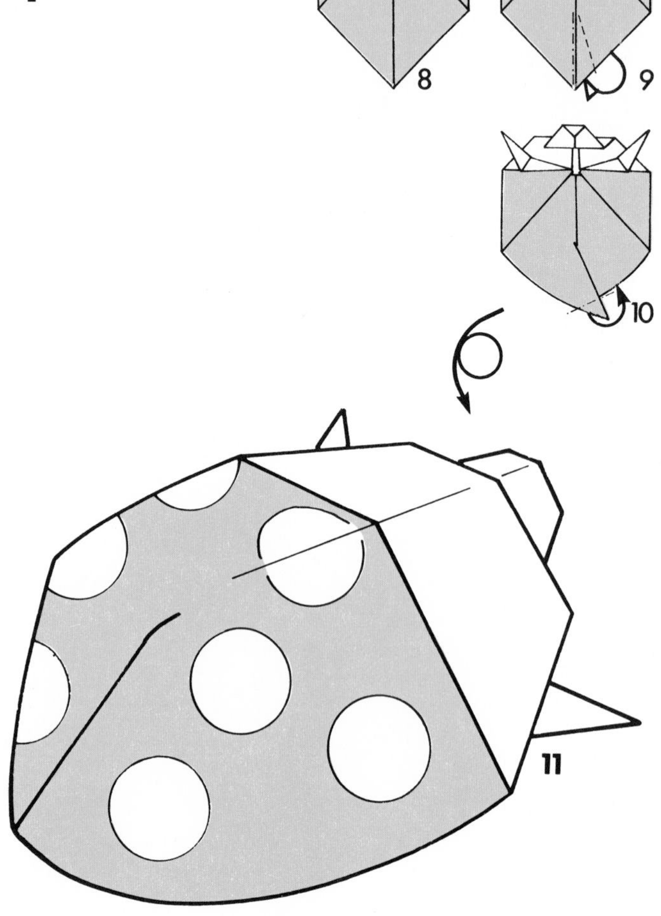

1 Fold the top edge to centre. Turn over.

2 Fold the bottom points to centre.

3 Fold left and right sides to centre.

4 Pull the inner corners of the square white flaps outwards and flatten.

5 Fold top left and right corners to centre.

6 Fold points up.

7 Rabbit-ear fold the two triangular flaps.

8 Fold top point down. Fold centre points outwards.

9 Pleat at top. Swivel at bottom and . . .

10 . . . tuck point into model behind. Turn over.

11 The ladybird completed.

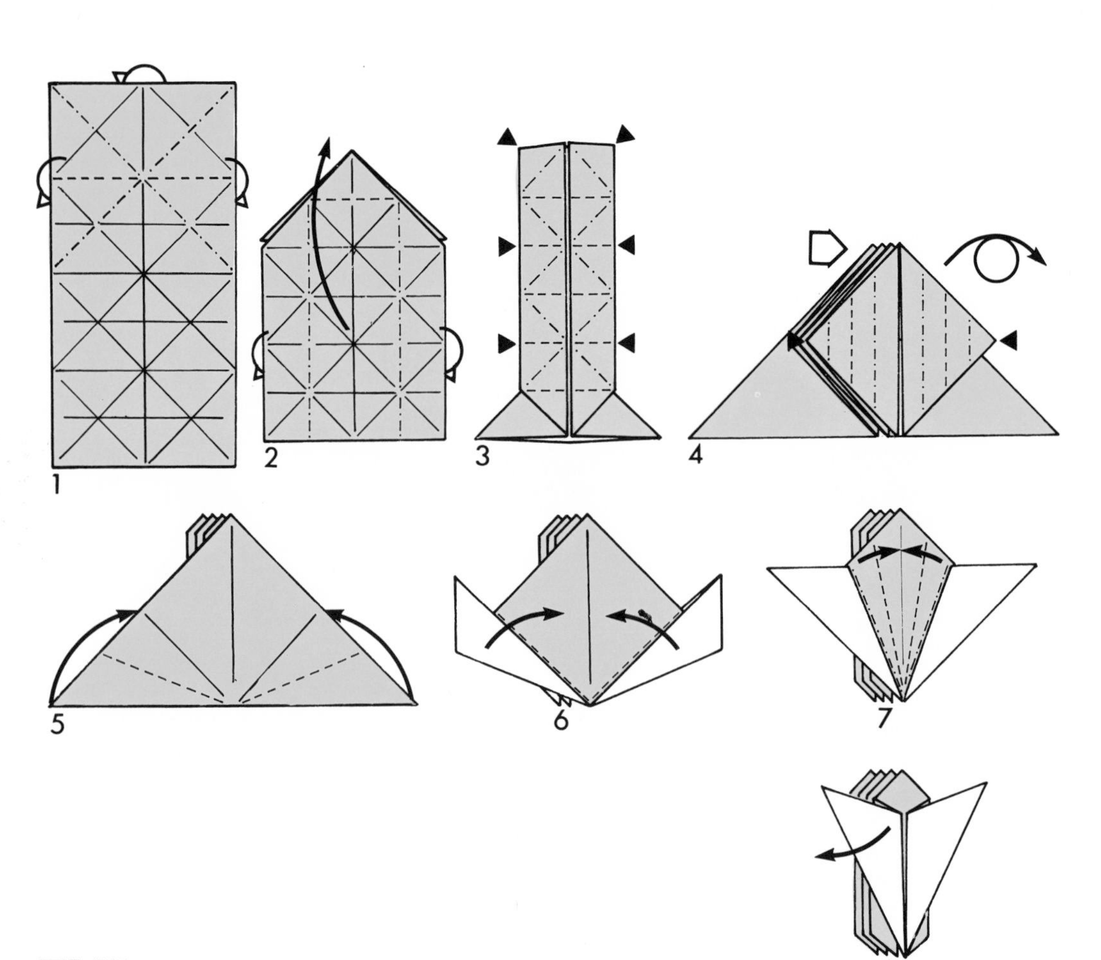

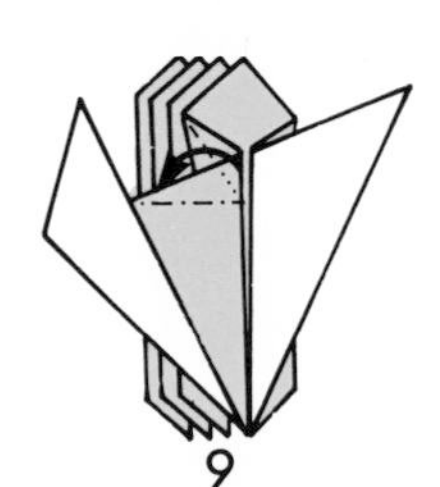

FLY (Max Hulme)

Use a large 2 × 1 rectangle of strong paper (foil backed paper is recommended), coloured side up. Crease as shown.

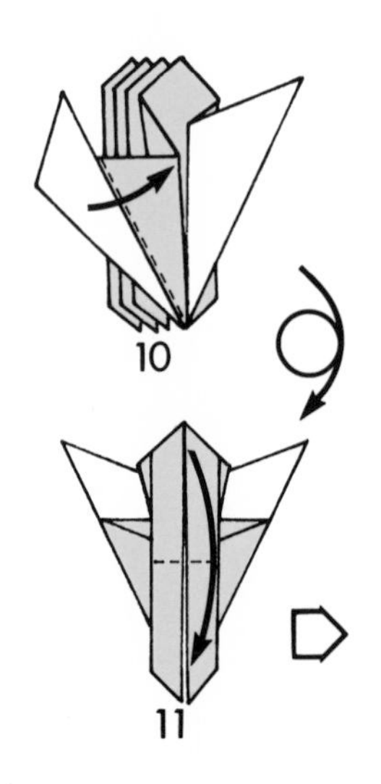

1 Collapse top of paper behind.

2 Fold up bottom edge, allowing sides of paper to come together at centre.

3 Push in folded edge at sides, raising six small triangular flaps . . .

4 . . . like this. Triple sink all six flaps. Turn over.

5 Outside reverse fold bottom edge to existing crease lines.

6 Fold over.

7 Swivel inner edges of white triangles to vertical centre line.

8 Partly unfold at left.

9 Swivel at left centre.

10 Fold at left. Repeat steps 8–10 on right flap; then turn over.

11 Fold down two flaps.

12 Flatten the bottom point. Mountain fold sides of upper flap at top.

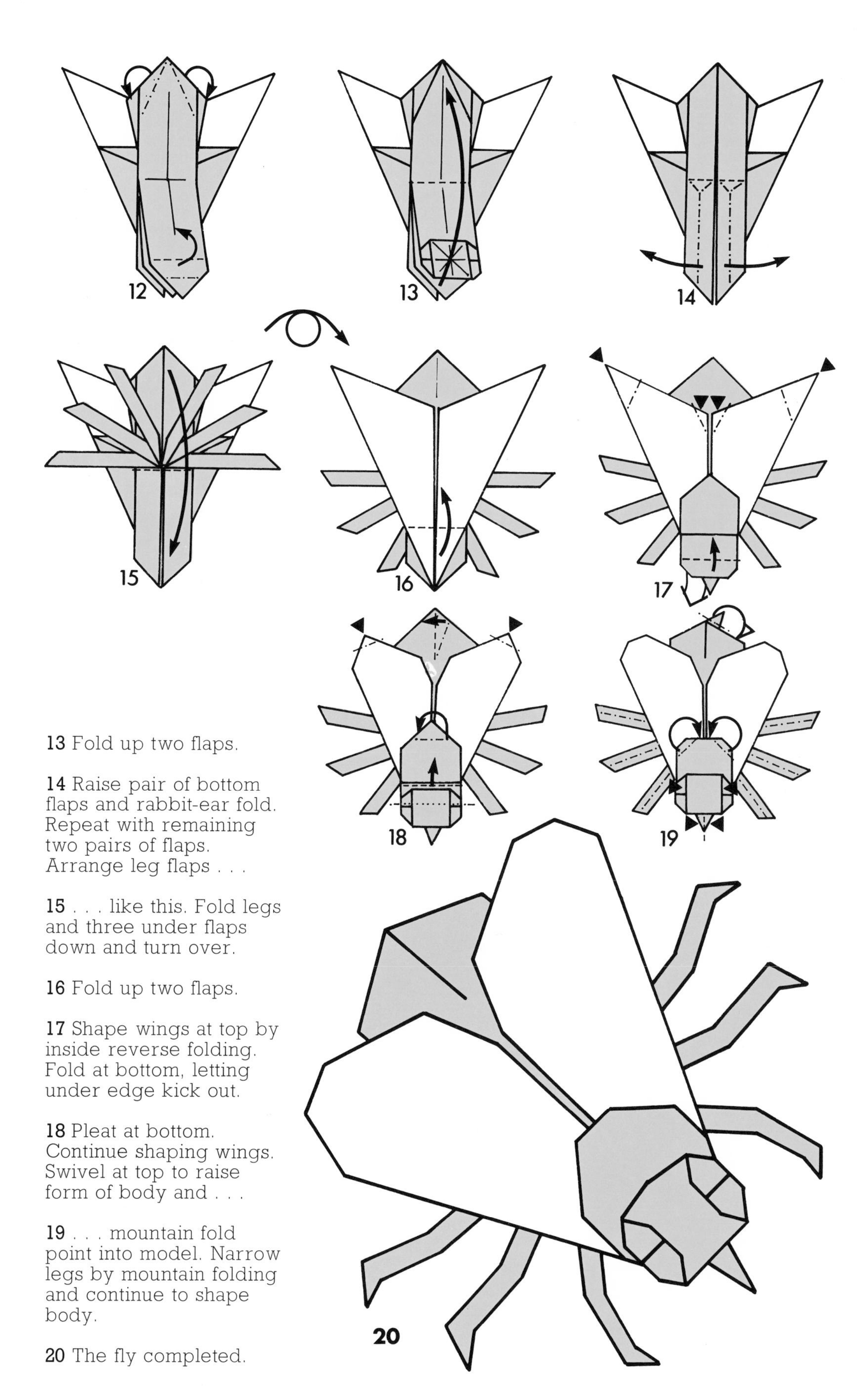

13 Fold up two flaps.

14 Raise pair of bottom flaps and rabbit-ear fold. Repeat with remaining two pairs of flaps. Arrange leg flaps . . .

15 . . . like this. Fold legs and three under flaps down and turn over.

16 Fold up two flaps.

17 Shape wings at top by inside reverse folding. Fold at bottom, letting under edge kick out.

18 Pleat at bottom. Continue shaping wings. Swivel at top to raise form of body and . . .

19 . . . mountain fold point into model. Narrow legs by mountain folding and continue to shape body.

20 The fly completed.

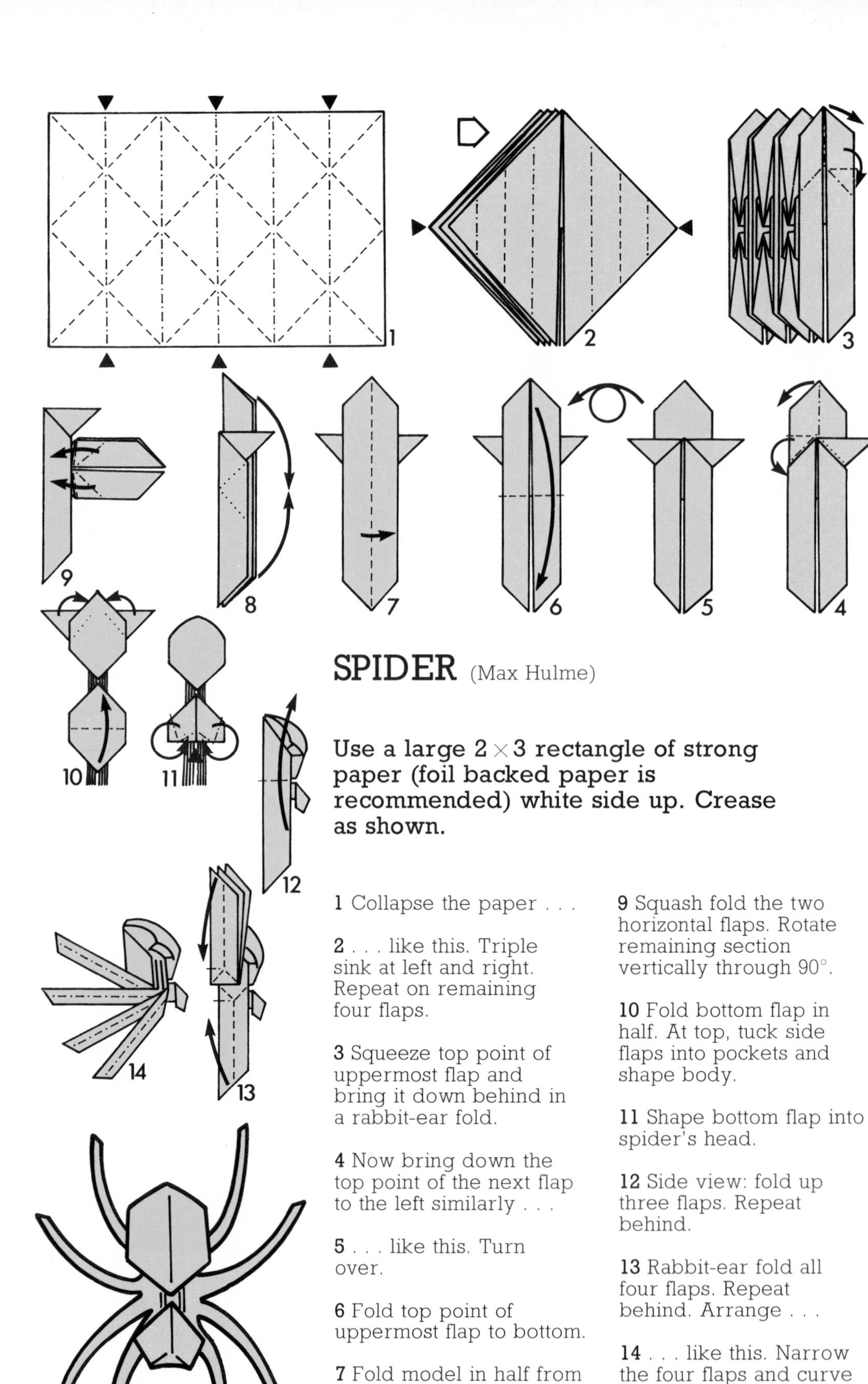

SPIDER (Max Hulme)

Use a large 2 × 3 rectangle of strong paper (foil backed paper is recommended) white side up. Crease as shown.

1 Collapse the paper . . .

2 . . . like this. Triple sink at left and right. Repeat on remaining four flaps.

3 Squeeze top point of uppermost flap and bring it down behind in a rabbit-ear fold.

4 Now bring down the top point of the next flap to the left similarly . . .

5 . . . like this. Turn over.

6 Fold top point of uppermost flap to bottom.

7 Fold model in half from left to right.

8 Inside reverse fold top and bottom points to right.

9 Squash fold the two horizontal flaps. Rotate remaining section vertically through 90°.

10 Fold bottom flap in half. At top, tuck side flaps into pockets and shape body.

11 Shape bottom flap into spider's head.

12 Side view: fold up three flaps. Repeat behind.

13 Rabbit-ear fold all four flaps. Repeat behind. Arrange . . .

14 . . . like this. Narrow the four flaps and curve to form legs. Repeat behind.

15 The spider completed.